Endorsements

Anthony is the real deal! His new book *'Hearing the Heart of Heaven'* contains biblical and practical tools for walking in healthy prophetic ministry. Having known Anthony for over 10 years I have seen his journey into prophetic ministry develop and mature and this book demonstrates that beautifully. His insights, practical responses and witty observations will help accelerate anyone on their journey in learning to hear God's voice clearly. The model of prophetic ministry in the church has often been punctuated with weak theology, bad character and unhelpful prophetic practices. Anthony skilfully helps reshape our thinking in these areas in order to liberate the church into a new season of authentic God-glorifying prophetic ministry. Pastors, leaders and new Christians alike should make this book a part of their spiritual formation in hearing God's voice. I certainly will be recommending his book in the many contexts I serve in. *'Hearing the Heart of Heaven'* will do you good. Read it!

Julian Adams,
Director of Frequentsee and Author of 'Kiss of the Father'
frequentsee.org

***

'Hearing the Heart of Heaven' is a book I have been waiting for and is a much-needed resource in the church today. Anthony Hilder gives clear biblical guidelines for the prophetic and its purpose for the church and the world. This book de-mystifies the gift and brings

practical and realistic application throughout. It clearly gives the dos and don'ts of bringing prophetic revelation, weighing and testing and how to lead prophetic people. If you are someone desiring the gift of prophecy, if you want to grow and mature in this gift, if you are a leader hungry for more of the presence of God, and you want to hear the heart of heaven for your church and city then let me, without hesitation, recommend this book, and its author, to you.

Andy Robinson
Senior Leader, Kings Church Horsham

Hearing The Heart of Heaven

Developing a Personal Prophetic Culture

Anthony Hilder

Scripture quotations are from The ESV® Bible (The Holy Bible, English Standard Version®), copyright © 2001 by Crossway, a publishing ministry of Good News Publishers. Used by permission. All rights reserved.

Front cover photo by Jannis Brandt on www.unsplash.com

First printing September 2018

ISBN 9781718144903

Visit anthonyhilder.com

For Katie, my bride.

All the best bits are because of you!

Thank you for the constant championing.

I love you.

What hinders me from hearing is that I am taken up with other things. It is not that I will not hear God, but I am not devoted in the right place. I am devoted to things, to service, to convictions, and God may say what He likes but I do not hear Him.

- Oswald Chambers, My Utmost for His Highest

Contents

Forewords

A book entitled 'Hearing the Heart of Heaven' takes on a broad remit, so it helps when I know the author well. He has worked for me and with me, so I know Anthony to be practical, theological, spiritual, funny, personable, and real. I was pleased to see all six of these characteristics flow throughout the book.

Firstly, 'Hearing the Heart of Heaven' is practical. One of the best examples of this is in the chapter entitled 'Speaking The King's English', where Anthony explains the 'ABCDE' of prophetic delivery. This simple yet brilliant practical advice provides an anchor point to help the learner grow in confidence. There are many other examples and every chapter ends with an invitation to a practical exercise to 'practice the prophetic'. I was definitely not disappointed in the practical element of this book. Anthony never teaches or writes without a goal of equipping and he has done a good job with this.

Secondly, 'Hearing the Heart of Heaven' is theological. Anthony delivers clear, concise and consistent references and expositions from scripture. His biblical knowledge means that he has done much of the hard work for us, making us hungrier to anchor our prophetic gifting and practice in the Bible. When you are with him, it is obvious that he has studied the Bible beyond the average but he always makes it accessible. This book, in particular, brings accessible theology in relation to the prophetic gift.

Thirdly, 'Hearing the Heart of Heaven' is spiritual. One of the things which I look for in spirituality is the ability to handle tension, the incomplete, and the not totally answerable or confirmable. The spiritual life isn't black and white and Anthony really helps the reader here, constantly pointing to the bigger picture rather than a finished short story. A book on prophecy by nature must be spiritual and this book will guide you into new depths even though there may not be concrete answers for every question.

Fourthly, 'Hearing the Heart of Heaven' is funny. Anthony has a great sense of humour and it is evident throughout the book. What I like though is that he uses his humour to create context and contrast. In several places, he articulates what we have probably felt but not found words for.

Fifthly, 'Hearing the Heart of Heaven' is personable. I most appreciate Anthony around the meal table. That is where all of his characteristics are brought together through his person-ability and this book has that element too. Despite some depth and theology, it is engaging and conversational. I encourage you to dialogue with this book, asking questions of it as if Anthony were around the table with you. As you read on you will probably find his responses.

Finally, 'Hearing the Heart of Heaven' is real. Real, honest, and even raw. The subject of hearing from heaven really needs a 'tell it the way it is' element. We can't allow the mystery and spiritual nature of the subject hide heresy or stupidity. Anthony clearly says that prophesying in part will mean that not everything we say will be correct. That's real and much needed. None of us can dare to risk infallibility in this or any other area of our Christian lives. In this way, he sets us all up for success, but with our characters intact.

Anthony loves to bring definition. In both the specifics, and in the overarching picture, he has done a great job of giving us definitions related to the subject, which make sense spiritually, practically & theologically. These definitions which will give you confidence as you pursue this gift in your life.

This is a book written by someone I know. Not only that, I trust him. Through 'Hearing the Heart of Heaven', Anthony has created a set of interactive lenses which are invaluable for anyone wanting to increase their capacity to hear heaven's voice.

Read, reread, discuss, investigate and practice. The world needs Heaven's voice and I believe that when we prophesy we enable an encounter for people with a God who knows the future. There are few things more precious than that.

Paul Manwaring
Senior Leadership Team , Bethel Church, Redding
paulmanwaring.com

***

Every Samuel needs an Eli. Read 1 Samuel 3. If you are on an adventure with the Holy Spirit then you will hear His voice. And, when you hear it, you will need a wise guide who can cut through all the cultural nonsense and help train you in the way you should proceed. A guide who can say, without pretension, "I know how to listen to the Lord. Let me help."

Anthony Hilder has been an Eli to me many times. His wisdom has changed my life. I heartily recommend this book to you and your people as we embark, together, on our adventure with the Holy Spirit.

Let me tell you about Anthony: he doesn't suffer fools gladly. He is forthright, direct and whip-smart. I suspect, like Eeyore, he is happiest when he has something to be grumpy about. But there is always a streak of humour running through his grump. Somehow this guy can smile and frown at the same time. Most people, like Anthony, can identify the absurd things churches do, but can we, like Anthony, love them anyway? A lot of us use our theology and biblical knowledge as a weapon against our enemies. But can we, like Anthony, use our intelligence to encourage our friends to better things? We may know a lot of 'prophets' who think their gift is about cutting people down to size. But do we know many people like Anthony who practice prophecy to strengthen, build-up and comfort? I do not know many people who can pinpoint with accuracy human folly and delusion and do it with love, kindness and humility, but Anthony somehow can.

I say "somehow", but, of course, it is not a mystery. Anthony is a guy who has spent a lot of time with the Master. Anthony hears Jesus well. He knows Jesus. He has spent a lot of time with Him, His words, and with other people who love Him. So when Anthony has something to say, I, for one, stop to listen.

This book is a case in point. Anthony's personality shines through on every page. You will not find here a tome of cobbled together Christian clichés. Anthony cuts through the chaff straight to the grain. This is a book on cultivating a prophetic culture that is practical, informed and no-nonsense. But it is not cynical. It is alive to the new things the Holy Spirit does and says. It knows that the Kingdom of Heaven breaks through all the time and in many places. It understands that the prophetic is a wild, exciting gift too fun, too biblically rooted and too real to be left just to sentimentalists, dry academics or crazy charismatics.

Eventually, every Eli will need a Samuel. As you proceed on your adventure with the Holy Spirit, you will find yourself in a position to guide others. You will grow in your faith and in your ability to disciple, encourage and upbuild the people around you. Anthony and his book can help with this too. It is an excellent resource. As you hear the heart of Heaven in your personal lives and communities, I prophesy that you, too, will be able to say without arrogance "follow me as I follow Christ."

Dr Stephen Backhouse
Dean of Theology for Local Church, Westminster Theology Centre
tentheology.com

Preface

During 2013, my wife Katie and I had the pleasure of being hosted for two months by a church in Noosa, Australia. Our time there was to be one of mutual benefit. For the church, we would work with them across a number of ministry areas with support and input, and for us, we would have the chance to experience, explore and enjoy one of the most unique countries in the world.

The two of us were asked by the senior leader of the church if we would lead a number of training sessions on the gift of prophecy. As our first joint teaching assignment, we worked together to create the content and arrived at a four-session course comprised of biblical teaching and practical exercises, which we called 'Prophetic Culture.'

The course was well received and a number of people asked us for copies of our presentation slides. Since that initial workshop, we taught the course a number of times elsewhere, including the United Kingdom and the United States. Each time, the content went through a number of evolutions, changes and tweaks   - additions, subtractions, refinements and restructuring.

Fast forward to 2015, and we were living in Redding, California. I was working as the Associate Pastor and C.O.O. of Global Legacy, which is the apostolic network of leaders connected to Bethel Church, Redding. Working under Paul Manwaring, we designed and delivered training programs for leaders across the world. One such program was the Leader Development Program, which focused on twelve essential leadership core values - one value per month. Each month honed in on the value, using required reading and listening as well as live webinars. Paul, others and I regularly taught different aspects of the course and it proved to be a popular program.

One of the core values was 'a prophetic lifestyle' and one day, the Program Manager, a good friend called Lara Hochstetler, approached me and asked me if I would write a training manual on the prophetic for that particular month. She had learned I had been teaching on the subject for a while, knew I wanted to write books one day and after speaking with Paul, proposed this opportunity to kickstart my process!

Over the next few months, whilst imbibing more coffee and cinnamon buns than any man should safely consume, the presentation slides were used as an outline and transformed into a manuscript for a training manual. Entitled 'Developing a Personal Prophetic Culture', the program participants gave positive feedback during 2015 and 2016, and all was well.

During this time, my daughter Sophie was born and my world turned upside down in a haze of sleeplessness, nappies and joy. The manuscript was put on hold during 2016, which was a year of learning to be a father. As 2017 entered the scene, it bought with it the beginning of our next significant process of transition. We said goodbye to our life in California and returned to the U.K, Katie pregnant in her third trimester and our material belongings packed up into storage. A few weeks after returning, my son Ross was born.

Halfway through 2018, I began to think about this manuscript collecting cyber dust on my laptop hard drive. I revisited it and added shorter chapters, more personal illustrations and examples, chapter introductions with which I tried to be funny - you can decide if I was successful - and the practical exercises at the end of each chapter. The manuscript changed into a book, and that brings me up to today, with my release date just over one week away.

One person might write a book, but more than one person is involved in its process. There are some people I want to thank for their input along the way.

Firstly, my wife Katie. Not only did she co-write the original prophetic training course content in 2013, but she read through the manuscript and continually made incredibly helpful suggestions. Thank you for being patient with me when I commit a grammatical faux pas, or when I've shown my frustration at learning I've got punctuation poverty yet again.

Secondly, Lara Hochstetler. It was her idea, suggestion, pursuing, nagging, chastising, challenging and heart to see people step into their dreams that kickstarted the journey of presentation to prose. Thank you for not accepting my excuses for how busy I was, or how bad I was, and getting this book out of me!

Thirdly, my 2016 Global Legacy interns: Miriam Melnichuk, Kewyn Appadoo, Gabriel Howley, and Bill Hartley - my first critiquing readers! I pretended that giving them my manuscript to read as an assignment was for their growth and development, but really it was so I could get some free feedback and input. Each of them was very kind and gentle in sharing thoughts, suggestions and improvements. Thank you for helping shape the work!

Finally, Brian Marriott and Santino Hamberis. Two of my longest standing friendships, and both wise men. They were the first people outside of my 'ministry circle' to read the manuscript and give feedback. Their exceptional encouragement and positivity helped give me confidence that maybe, just maybe, I had something to say that was worth putting in print. Thank you, gentlemen, for supporting me.

My hope is that this book acts as a springboard for readers in both knowledge and practice, and is a helpful signpost in the journey of growing in the prophetic gifts.

Anthony Hilder
August 2018

Acknowledgements

The preface contains thanks for people who have been instrumental in directly shaping this book, but I wanted to acknowledge some people who have been key in shaping me, and therefore, this book indirectly.

Firstly, I want to thank John Groves. As the first senior leader I sat under and learned from, you set the reference point that I've always compared every other leader too! I'm blessed that you set such an incredible example. At the start of my journey of faith, as I sat under your teaching as a teenager Sunday by Sunday, you demonstrated the importance of knowing the scriptures to me. You showed me why I should bring my life and beliefs under the authority of the Bible, and was kind and patient with me as I navigated doubts, sin, stupidity and being a young man with lots to say, but only some of it actually any good! Thank you.

Secondly, I want to thank Steve Brading. You showed me what anointed, healthy and humbly submitted prophetic ministry should look like in a local church. Anchored in the scriptures yet not lacking in power, your teaching and example shaped my understanding then and still does, to this day. Being part of that men's group around your kitchen table, firing questions at you (and probably arguing!) I learned how to hear God for myself, and for others. Thank you.

Thirdly, I want to thank Paul Manwaring. You've been a spiritual father in my life who opened doors for me and gave me a platform that in the natural, I shouldn't have had any right to. You've shaped my thinking in the area of leadership and creativity immensely. I've always felt welcomed and championed by you, not just in ministry but in my personal life too. Thank you for everything - the love, the generosity, the advice, the support, the excellent scones, wine and coffee - and for writing such a nice foreword!

Introduction

In the New Testament, we are introduced to the church in the city of Corinth. The Apostle Paul had quite the involvement with them, writing at least twice[1] to help teach and train them. Corinth as a city was very cosmopolitan. It was a melting pot of cultures, ethnicities, religions and livelihoods. Because of where the city was located, it became a key trading hub. A place of hustle and bustle, action and activity, it seems that the church there followed in a similar vein - full of clamour, noise and action. Paul's letters to the Corinthian church show us that it wasn't exactly short of demonstrations of signs, wonders and prophecy. In fact, it sounds like their meetings were a bit of a free-for-all and Paul has to give them instructions to sit down, shut up, control themselves, and actually listen to one another! If the ancient Greco-Roman world had them available, you could almost bet the Corinthians would splash out on white power suits, big backcombed hair, banners with pictures of rainbows, and other 1970s Christian charismatic paraphernalia.

It is interesting that Paul never tries to shut down the expression of spiritual power but instead, encourages the Corinthians to be loving whilst still use the gifts. He tells them to 'pursue love, and eagerly desire the spiritual gifts, especially that you may prophesy.'[2] In our desire to grow in the prophetic, love and hunger are meant to be partnered.

---

[1] 1 and 2 Corinthians

[2] 1 Corinthians 14:1

This leads me to ask two questions. Firstly, how can we do that? An interesting word in the verse is 'especially'. Paul elevates prophecy, highlighting it over other giftings of the Holy Spirit. This leads to my second question: why does he do that?

This book is an examination of those two questions. To do this, the book will consist of three sections.

The first section is entitled 'Prophetic Definition' and answers the question 'what is prophecy?' The word, in our modern culture, has come to mean knowing the future. Are those who prophesy meant to be like Nostradamus, knowing all that is to come, and being able to predict the winning lottery numbers week by week? Or is prophecy, according to the Bible, something else?

The second section is called 'Prophetic Structure' and answers the question 'how does prophecy work?' If God does indeed talk to those He loves, what does He sound like? How do I know when it is God speaking, and not voices in my head, or the additives in my unusually coloured breakfast cereal?

The third and final section is called 'Prophetic Character' and answers the question 'what is our part in the process of prophecy?' Do we have responsibilities, or do we just open our mouth like we are catching flies and expect God to fill it with divine words of such profound wisdom that all weep around us? Spoiler alert: if you think this, you might develop jaw ache after a while.

I've entitled the book 'Hearing The Heart of Heaven' because, simply put, that is a very basic understanding of both what prophecy is, and what its purpose is. Prophecy is simply hearing the heart of Heaven - what God thinks and feels. When I prophesy, it is so others can hear the heart of Heaven.

The subtitle of 'Developing A Personal Prophetic Culture' is not meant to be a collection of charismatic buzzwords, but in my mind communicates a number of things. Firstly, if we want to prophesy well we need to **develop** elements within ourselves. There is a process of growth involved. Secondly, since this development has to be **personal**, it means that there must be an impact inside us first if we want to see impact outside of us through our ministry. How can we change the world if we don't let our world be changed? Thirdly, the definition of terms is always helpful. Let's make sure we understand what **prophecy** is and does - there are some 'interesting' ideas out there! Fourthly, our **culture** is the external evidence of our internal values. Simply put, it is our beliefs consistently demonstrated through our behaviours. What we believe shapes what we do. We'll examine key values connected to healthy prophetic demonstration, so we can cultivate them, absorb them into our lives, and live in a way that naturally acts as a conduit for hearing the heart of Heaven, irrespective of the frequency or accuracy of our prophetic words.

I hope you've seen that the title is in the present tense. It is a journey, an ongoing pilgrimage of discovery and growth. We should always be 'hearing' and 'developing' because we never arrive. We should never say 'I've got this, thanks very much!' Scripture tells us that we always, always, always 'prophesy in part'.[3] On its own, this truth would be discouraging. Yet the Bible gives us many instances of truths in tension so we are still encouraged to eagerly desire the gift.

[3] 1 Corinthians 13:9

Let's be the hungriest and healthiest prophetic people we can be as we walk this road together.

To help us do this, I've included some practical exercises at the end of each chapter called 'Practising the Prophetic.' Each exercise takes what has just been covered and grounds it into our daily lives. It's great to have a good theology of prophecy, but if our theology isn't practised then we actually have a bad theology! Good beliefs convert to good behaviour and so it's important to have a good practice of prophecy too. My recommendation is that after each chapter, you implement the exercise before returning to continue the book. I believe you'll get the most impact, and therefore growth, from doing so.

My prayer for you is that, like me, you would learn, grow and develop this gift today, tomorrow and in future years all whilst never feeling like you've arrived, matured or become an expert. The gift of prophecy, like all spiritual gifts, anointings, mantles, coverings and other buzzwords, isn't actually for us - it's for those around us. God gives us gifts because we're meant to use them for the benefit of others.

A successful outworking of this book would be people looking to bless others with the words of God that help them continue to walk this walk of faith we've all been bought into. We need to be a prophetic people because His words change everything, and He still has a lot to say. Ultimately, once God has spoken, everything else becomes commentary. Hearing the heart of Heaven brings us into the divine dialogue.

PART I
PROPHETIC
DEFINITION

I used to be on a debating team. I wish I could say it was because I had a deep passion for learning and truth, as well as a desire to see solutions to complex social, political and global problems. The reality is that I loved having an excuse to miss school lessons to travel all over the country, try and impress girls by sneaking in poor quality alcohol, mock rich kids, and every so often stand in front of a group of people and say funny things into a microphone.

My headmaster, however, had a different idea and focused his attention on me. I'm sure he neglected the entire team, and indeed the whole school, for that matter, to pick on me. At least, that's what it felt like that to my overactive teenage mind. He would give me hard assignments. Things I actually had to read. Topics I needed to research and write position papers on. I had to debate and present views and opinions that I didn't believe in, which was really annoying, because I couldn't just turn up and say whatever tumbled into my brain. I had to **work**, pah!

Looking back now, I'm actually thankful. He saw something within me that I didn't, and he encouraged me in this area. At least, I tell myself that. Maybe he just wanted to give me a workload that forced me into the library and gave him some peace and quiet. But I suspect it was the former. Because through his teaching, training, mentoring and threats of detention, I began to act on his repeated encouragements and take things more seriously. When I won my first prize, he celebrated with me. No-one was more shocked than me to actually win something for talking, but he hid his shock equally well and continued celebrating and provoking me to be all I could be as the second, third and more prizes came in. He was very patient with me as I no doubt become insufferably cocky and arrogant but thanks to him, I grew into someone I would never have otherwise. I developed skills and abilities that have served me well in my subsequent years. It all started with words of encouragement because he saw me in a way I did not see myself. This is an illustration of what prophecy is and can do.

For some, prophecy has an element of mystery or mysticism about it. Some might think about tea-leaves or crystal balls. Others might have mental trauma from people frothing at the mouth whilst shouting in Shakespearean verse about a God of love who will smite them from the Earth. Some of us might even hear the word 'prophecy' and interpret that to mean oddballs who take glittery scissors and crayons to the Bible, cutting out and pasting in things in the Bible to change what it says.

I don't mean any of these things. In this first section, I will look at what prophecy is biblically, using, you know, the Bible funnily enough, and I'll dispel some of the Christian mythology that surrounds it. All without frothing at the mouth or using Shakespearean verbiage.

1. Divine Testimony

Prophecy is a spiritual gift - one of many - that God gives the church. Spiritual gifts are abilities that God gives to Christians to harness His power and benefit others around them. There are a couple of lists in the Bible and some gifts seem pretty impressive. Miracles! Healings! Leadership! Others are more mundane and a lot less sexy. Helps - notice, no exclamation mark. Giving. Administration. On a side note, celibacy and martyrdom are also spiritual gifts and I can promise you that the only prayers I've prayed about those gifts are that God **wouldn't** give them to me.

The point is, though, that God is interested in the ordinary details of life, and living life in a supernatural and loving way. So whilst the seeming boring gifts seem, well, pointless, they are in fact key in doing life well. The more spectacular gifts remind us that as Christians, we do represent a supernatural God not of this world who loves to intervene. Here is another example of truth in tension - we need to live naturally supernatural, and supernaturally natural. This isn't just cute wordplay, but the tension of living with a foot in two worlds. We err equally if we ignore the supernatural as we do if we overlook the natural.

Coming back to the gift of prophecy, Paul lists it within 1 Corinthians 12:4-11 and Romans 12:4-8. Both passages are pretty clear that it is a gift. God is the gift-giver and gives according to His choice. So no-one really can boast about something given to them for free. That's fine, but what is this gift of prophecy? Should it enable me to know what stocks and shares I can buy ahead of time in order to become a zillionaire?

Elsewhere, we're told that 'the testimony of Jesus is the spirit of prophecy'.[4] In a court of law, a witness would take the stand. They are called a witness because they *witnessed* something. They are questioned about the incident by a lawyer, or a barrister if you prefer the British version with the cool black robes and grey wig, and the witness literally says what they saw. This account is called a *testimony.* So this scripture tells us that prophecy is the testimony of Jesus *saying what he sees*. When we prophesy, we are saying what Jesus tells us He sees about a person or a situation.

Our own view of God will certainly influence or colour this, which is why all prophetic people should be students of scripture. If we believe that God is angry and judgemental then our words will reflect that. It is equally true that if we believe God is a good God, happy and loving and full of mercy to give second chances, then our words will reflect that.

If prophecy reveals to us *what* Jesus sees, it follows that it also shows us *how* He sees something. Paul told the Corinthians 'the one who prophesies speaks to people for their upbuilding, encouragement and consolation'.[5] This shows us the heart of Jesus: what He says to people is for the purpose of strengthening them. We can see that prophecy reveals to us the heart and mind of God - what He thinks and what He feels. This verse in 1 Corinthians 14:3 gives us a threefold purpose of prophecy.

---

[4] Revelation 19:10

[5] 1 Corinthians 14:3

Firstly, the Greek word translated 'upbuilding'[6] is a word meaning 'building, construction, a physical edifice.' It is derived from two words: the first meaning 'house'[7] and the second meaning 'housetop'[8]. The image suggested is adding to a house by building an extension, or increasing the capacity by raising the roof. One goal of prophecy is to speak words of life and hope that build up and increase the hearer's spiritual strength and size.

Secondly, 'encouragement' is a Greek word *paraklesis* which, at its root, includes the concepts of coming alongside a person, and calling someone by their name. Putting these two ideas together, we could say that to encourage another is to recognise who someone truly is and walk alongside them whilst 'calling their name' - reminding them to tell them their true identity, who they are and who they are meant to be. Interestingly, this is one of the roles of Holy Spirit, who is called the *parakletos* - the Helper - in John 14, 15 and 16. Encouragement is a huge deal in the Kingdom of God because it is a root of prophecy and a function of Holy Spirit.

Thirdly, 'consolation'[9] comes from a word containing the concepts of coming alongside, and speaking words of comfort and calm. It suggests elements of tenderness and support, like someone who runs up to a flagging marathon runner to reassure, bring water and bring hope to keep going.

---

[6] Oikodome, Strong's 3619

[7] Oikos, Strong's 3624

[8] Doma, Strong's 1430

[9] Paramuthia, Strong's 3889

Therefore, we see a threefold function of prophecy: firstly, prophecy should strengthen the recipient; secondly, it should fill them with courage and faith as they are reminded of how God sees them; thirdly, it should comfort them and bring hope in tough times.

As well as these three functions, the prophetic ministry reveals two things that are hidden - God's purposes in the present, and His plans for the future. We could call the revelation of what He is doing in the here and now *forthtelling,* and the disclosure of the future could be termed *foretelling.* Because the prophetic reveals what Jesus sees, we can expect mysteries to be unveiled in the hearts of those receiving prophecy.

This is why Paul tells the Corinthian church that unbelievers should be impacted by the potency of the prophetic ministry and convicted of sin because the secrets of their hearts are revealed.[10] Because of the three-fold function of prophecy I mentioned earlier, I don't take these secrets to be their private sins - I don't believe prophecy functions like a microphone, blurting out a list of all the bad thoughts, actions and attitudes of an individual for all to hear. Public shaming by believers of others isn't congruent with upbuilding, encouragement or consolation. Rather, I think these verses are talking about the concept of forthtelling. If a person's hopes, dreams and passions, known only to them, are told to them by a stranger who claims to be hearing a message from God for them, I would expect some kind of reaction! At least, the possibility of an increased awareness of God being there. One such response to that increased awareness could be a repentance and conversion.

---

[10] 1 Corinthians 14:24-25

The prophetic is not just for the 'there and then' of the future. It is also for the 'here and now' of the present. It is a spiritual metal-detector, discovering the gold hidden by the Lord within the hearts of people so it can be uncovered and enjoyed by all.

Practising The Prophetic

We've just seen that the prophetic gifts have three functions: upbuilding, encouragement and consolation, as outlined above. Ask God to show you three people in your life - one to 'build up', one to encourage, and another to bring hope to. Go to each of them and be an 'upbuilder', encourager and hope-bringer respectively. If you don't know what to say, ask God - but don't worry about prophesying. If you don't know what to say, just say something positive and affirming! Right now, it's more important that you are a strength-bringer, courage-giver, and comforter.

2. Covenants & Kings

The prophetic ministry is shown in both testaments in our Bible. We see demonstrations of prophets in both the Old and New Testaments, and they seem to be very different! The Old Testament prophet seems to call down fire from Heaven, speak words of judgement and warning to God's people and the surrounding nations, have bizarre visions, or even carry out strange prophetic acts such as cooking food over animal dung[11] or marrying a prostitute[12]. Yet there is none of this in the prophetic ministry in the New Testament, which seems to have a very different flavour. Why is this?

In the same vein, it seems that some people who feel they are prophets model themselves on biblical prophets, which seems like a good idea, admittedly. But they almost always seem to choose the vilifying, judgemental, rebuking style of ministry they see, which doesn't line up with the New Testament teaching of the prophetic - building up, encouraging and comforting. I'm not sure about you, but being told that God wants to smite me and so will firebomb my house with meteors from Heaven because I went to a party last night isn't going to make me feel warm and cuddly inside.

The role of the prophetic ministry has changed because we are now living in a new and better covenant. We must interpret the teachings and examples of the old covenant through a new covenant lens. In some cases, this actually overrides certain aspects of the former

[11] Ezekiel 4

[12] Hosea 1

covenant, with elements of the prophetic ministry being one such case. It seems foolish to live and minister in an Old Testament mentality when we should have a New Testament mindset. But if you are going to follow the Old Testament model, at least be theologically consistent and stop eating bacon whilst you embrace all the rules in Leviticus. Then go and read Galatians and Hebrews, both of which have a lot to say about the role of the Old Testament Law in the lives of the Christian, until you find yourself quoting them in your sleep.

Let's compare the Old Testament model and the New Testament model and see just how different they really are.

Old Testament Prophecy

Moses shared some thoughts about the role of the prophet. He was a prophet himself, so would certainly be an authority on hearing from God. He wrote:

'But the prophet who presumes to speak a word in My Name that I have not commanded him to speak, or who speaks in the name of other gods, that same prophet shall die... When a prophet speaks in the name of the Lord, if the word does not come to pass or come true, that is a word that the Lord has not spoken; the prophet has spoken it presumptuously.'[13]

Under the old covenant, the bar for prophetic accuracy was set very high: 100%. That's right, total prophetic perfection. No off-days. No half-right words. Hitting the nail on the head, on the money, every single time. This is because of the nature of the Mosaic covenant, which was a covenant of law. The people were judged by God on

---

[13] Deuteronomy 18:20-22

account of what they did - their works. The Commandments summarise the Law and set the standard for a righteous life, and they had to follow those instructions to the letter. Blessings and curses were conditional depending on the success of the people in obeying what God had established. If they did well, God would bless them. If they didn't do well, God would judge them. This arrangement shows us the context of the prophet's role in that covenant: they were the covenant enforcers, sent by God to bring warnings of judgement when the people strayed. They would come to remind the people to turn back to God through the keeping of the law.

If you are familiar with the overarching story of the Bible, you'll see a recurring pattern in the Old Testament. Time and again, the people of God enjoy God's blessing but then become complacent, embracing sin and compromise through idolatry and sexual immorality. God, in His kindness, sends a prophetic voice to them to warn them to repent, but the people (or the representative of the people, such as their king) refuse to listen. The judgement God had warned them about comes about, aimed at bringing them to repentance and therefore back into a healthy relationship with God. The nation turns back to God, and He blesses them. Repeat that a fair few times until the patience of God finally runs out about a thousand or so years after He initially gave the people His Law. This time, God's judgement comes in the form of the Assyrian and Babylonian empires destroying Israel and Judah, including the temple - the house of God - whilst the people are exiled and taken away as slaves. They lose all the things that promised to them in the Old Covenant that marked them out as God's people, which include the promised land, the temple and God's protection. That seems harsh. Isn't God a God of mercy, forgiveness and kindness? Yes, He is, and that is why the Exile was actually an act of mercy, which also shows us the role of the prophetic voice. The prophets begin speaking, saying that God wants to create a New Covenant written on the hearts of his people so that they would all know Him[14]. We begin to see prophetic foretelling of the new and better covenant Christ created for us.

Now, imagine you are a king. Not a modern day king, although that would still be rather nice. An old-school king, when your reign was unquestioned and your opinions never disputed. Which is even better. You're quite happy with your big gold crown, everyone telling you how amazing you are, and when you ask for anything you want, someone will get it for you. You might be a nice king or an evil king. Either way, as a king, you have things to do and people to rule. You have quite a responsibility. Now imagine you are the king of the people of God: you'd have a pretty clear job description and example to set. Picture someone coming into your royal court and telling you God isn't impressed with you, your attitude or what you've been doing, and He wants you to repent or He is going to judge you. All said, publicly, in front of your closest advisors. Chances are, you wouldn't be impressed and would want to make an example of this upstart who dares presume to speak for God against you, the very king who God Himself chose!

Now, switch roles. Imagine you are the prophet, told by God to go to an evil king and publicly admonish him to change his ways because God is displeased with him. It doesn't seem like the kind of job any sane, rational, balanced person would volunteer for. Yet this scenario was the reality of the role of the prophet in the Old Testament. They wouldn't necessarily be the most popular figures in society, certainly not according to the ruling figures! Consider the messages of

[14] Jeremiah 31:31-34

prophets like Jonah, Jeremiah and Isaiah, for example, who all called nations and kings to account. Imagine how their social standing would plummet as they rebuked the people for whom they worshipped (idolatry), how they were living sexually (immorality) and how they were treating the poor (social justice.) These three themes of idolatry, immorality and social justice are repeated throughout the Old Testament because God cares about each one and interestingly, these are the areas that first begin to slide into compromise when individuals and nations turn their hearts away from Him.

To be called a prophet in the Old Testament was a significant thing, reflected by the high expectation of prophetic accuracy. If you claimed to speak for God, then said something that didn't come to pass, you lost all credibility and authority before kings and people. But ultimately and more importantly, so did God. Hence the risk of death for those presuming to speak for Him. Being a prophet in the Old Testament was a much bigger deal then printing business cards and setting up a website. This is why, for many of the prophets, the call of God was incredible and fearsome, laden with visions and encounters of breathtaking enormity. Isaiah saw God in the temple; Ezekiel saw living creatures that he could not describe; Jeremiah was called as a young man with a very clear conversation; Elisha saw Elijah taken to Heaven in a chariot of fire. You had to really know you were called by God because you risked death by speaking the truth of the word of God to kings, in the way Elijah and Jeremiah did. If you were called to be a prophetic covenant enforcer, then you had to know God was with you, otherwise, you would tremble before angry kings and fearfully remain silent whilst the very words of Heaven burned unsaid in your spirit.

New Testament Prophecy

Because the nature of the new covenant is different from the old covenant, it follows that the nature and role of the prophetic ministry must also be different. One of the most striking differences between the covenants is that the old was all about works, but the new is all about grace. When we unpack this, we can see that in a strange way, the new is also about works, but instead of our works, it is about the works of Christ. He worked for us, on our behalf, and we receive His righteousness and reward as a result. That's why it is a covenant of grace - God's unmerited kindness shown to us even though we do not deserve such kindness or blessing. On the Cross, Jesus declared, "It is finished!"[15] The word translated 'finished' here is a Greek word, *tetelestai*, which is an accounting term that means 'paid in full.' Jesus is proclaiming that the sin-debt of humanity is settled in full, and there is now a clean ledger, a zero-sum bill, between God and Man. He paid the debt that we could not so that we could access the blessings we previously could not. That's why the Gospel is such good news! We get what we could never get because of what Another did!

Jesus told His followers that He didn't come to abolish the law and the prophets, but actually came to fulfil them.[16] He was saying that the demands of the law, which dictated what was acceptable to God and what was not, i.e. what was righteous and unrighteous, were totally fulfilled by His life. On one level, this was confirmation that Christ never sinned, hence His sin-payment on behalf of us was acceptable. After all, how can you pay another's sin-debt if you yourself have contributed to it? But on another level, by living

---

[15] John 19:30

[16] Matthew 5:17

totally and utterly righteously, He met the standards demanded by a Holy God so had something He could give to us. At the Cross, a great exchange took place: Jesus took our sin from us and gave us His righteousness, which can never be lost or taken away.

This means that the judgement of God was poured out on Christ, who received the penalty of sin in our place as a substitute. Under the old covenant, the prophet was the spokesman who declared the coming judgement of God. In the new covenant, the judgement of God has already come and fallen on Christ. If we are in Him, we need not fear the judgement of God. Paul told the Romans that 'there is now no condemnation for those in Christ Jesus.'[17] The new covenant of grace means that God is pleased with us because as believers, we are the righteousness of God.[18] Not *have*; we *are*! It is our actual identity; not a garment that can be snatched away. It is the righteousness of God, who is always righteous. It is not the righteousness of man that becomes dull and smeared with the accumulation of the stain of sin.

So we see that prophecy always reveals the heart of God. His heart is a heart of grace, seeking to give to His people what they truly need. Under the old covenant, He gave the people the opportunity to repent again and again. In the new covenant, the opportunity for intimacy is given, again and again. This reiterates why the prophetic in this age is to build up, encourage and comfort.[19] New covenant prophecy is less about judgement and more about encouragement. A basis of love, as opposed to accuracy, is the measure of new covenant

---

[17] Romans 8:1

[18] 2 Corinthians 5:21

[19] 1 Corinthians 14:3

prophecy. Of course, we want accuracy, but primarily the scriptures show us the purpose of prophecy is love. An unloving prophetic word, according to New Testament standards, is a misnomer.

Next time you hear or see someone prophesying the forthcoming wrath of God on a sinful world, as they detail a people or place that God will smite with fire, consider that the heart of God in the new covenant is demonstrated through love; that prophecy is meant to build up, encourage and comfort; and that scripture teaches us that it is God's kindness that leads us to repentance.[20] Then ask if what you are seeing or hearing is an appropriate demonstration of the prophetic role in the new covenant. In this example, I would suggest that what you are experiencing is an irrelevant, ineffective and therefore potentially harmful attempt to minister in the Name of The Lord.

Interestingly, to those who would minister in this old covenant model, to be theologically consistent they need to take on the standards of that model. Which means submitting every single prophetic utterance to the standard of 100% accuracy, and accepting the penalty for anything less, which is execution through stoning[21]. Telling people off on God's behalf isn't as much fun now, is it?

Practising The Prophetic

We've seen that prophecy should be in the spirit of New Testament, wrapped up in love, and not in an Old Testament fire-and-brimstone

---

[20] Romans 2:4

[21] Deuteronomy 18:20-22

heart. Spend some time searching your heart about whether the loving, encouraging prophecy is the time of prophetic ministry you want to be involved with. If it is, pray a short prayer of dedication to God, dedicating your heart and mouth to be conduits of love to those He would have you prophesy to.

3. Healthy Prophets

Despite some teaching that floats around, prophecy is not a gift reserved only for the few special and super-spiritual ones. That is an Old Testament model, which the New Testament supersedes. Paul's letter was to a group of people, therefore his instructions and teachings should always be understood in the plural. Hence when he tells the Corinthians (who clearly need a lot of teaching!) that 'you can *all* prophesy one by one, so that *all* may learn and *all* may be exhorted'[22], he isn't limiting the number of prophetic people. He is being inclusive, not exclusive. His earlier exhortation to 'eagerly desire spiritual gifts, especially prophecy'[23] is addressed to the whole church, not just the spiritual superstars contained therein. Prophecy is meant to be a gift accessible to all so that all can hear God themselves on behalf of others. If we don't understand this, we will elevate those with the gift to an unhelpful place and create first and second-class Christians. That's a bad idea and creates division - another thing the Corinthians were pretty good at doing.

It was always the plan of God for His people to be prophetic. Remember, being prophetic isn't about having prophecies - it is about revealing the heart of God. Peter, preaching his super-sermon in Acts 2 that results in an altar-call response of three-thousand, quotes the prophet Joel when he declares that 'in the last days God will pour forth of His Spirit on all flesh; and your sons and your

---

[22] 1 Corinthians 14:31

[23] 1 Corinthians 14:1

daughters shall prophesy'.[24] Neither age nor gender nor spiritual maturity is a barrier to prophesying. God wants to speak *to* all people, and *through* all people.

This raises some interesting possibilities. Because prophecy is a gift and not an award, it may mean some surprising people prophesy! Because gifts are given according to the will of God and not in response to our performance, not only can we not earn it, but we also can't *un*-earn it! Therefore prophecy isn't a demonstration of spiritual maturity. Spiritual maturity is expressed through our fruit, not our gifts. The quality of our Christlike character reveals our maturity so the most immature or newest believer may prophesy incredibly. That's both amazing and humbling and should reinforce to us the incredible kindness and grace of God, who gives all of us things we don't deserve again and again.

Our character quibbles or sin also don't invalidate prophecy. Gifting should never excuse poor lifestyle choices, nor should poor lifestyle choices negate gifting. We are all works in progress, being sanctified from glory to glory. My point is that prophecy is not an indication of character or maturity, and vice-versa. Gifting is God showing Himself *through* us, but fruit is God showing Himself *in* us.

Like all talents and gifts, both natural and spiritual, there are different levels of ability. Whilst anyone can prophesy, not everyone does. There is always the potential though because God speaks to all His children. When someone prophesies consistently, we could say that they have a prophetic gift. If someone has a gift that seems to be expressed more frequently, with greater accuracy and authority, and people are blessed by it, we could say that they have a **prophetic**

---

24 Acts 2:17, citing Joel 2:28

ministry. These would be the people that have respect and listening ears primed when they come to share. Comparison isn't the point here - it isn't about levels or placings on some kind of prophetic league table. I merely wanted to highlight growth, and how we can identify different levels of gifting. So if we've identified someone with a prophetic ministry, does that mean they are a prophet? In fact, what is a prophet? Is someone who prophesies a prophet?

One time, I became aware of a gentleman who considered himself to be a prophet. He had a very interesting approach to prayer. Whenever he prayed publicly, whether it was to a group of three, thirty or three hundred, he always concluded his prayer with the phrase "I pray this as a prophet ordained and anointed by the Lord Jesus Christ". It was kind of awkward because it felt more like he was telling us rather than letting us make up our own minds. Unfortunately, it seems that today in the church the word 'prophet' has become a title in a way it was never intended to be. If we prophesy, does that make us a prophet? As in my friend's case, who decides who is a prophet? Do we? Do others? Does Jesus? As our starting place, let's examine what scripture says about prophets.

The first thing to note is that sometimes we can get our theology of the prophets *primarily* from the Old Testament. I'm not saying that the Old Testament shouldn't inform and shape our understanding - it is inspired scripture, after all - but we live in New Testament times. The Apostle Paul tells the Corinthians that the events of the Old Testament are examples and warnings to us,[25] and he tells the Roman church that the Old Testament contains examples for our teaching

---

[25] 1 Corinthians 10:11

and encouragement.[26] Our first step in building our theology about anything is to always look through the lens of the New Testament. That includes our view of the Old Testament and what it teaches, as well. So to understand biblical theology about prophets, we need to know what the New Testament teaches about prophets and let that shape our understanding, as well as what we see in the Old Testament.

Paul, in his letter to the Ephesians, talks about prophets as one of a group of 'five-fold ministries'. His words give some insight into the definition and role of prophets:

'When He [Christ] ascended on high He led a host of captives and He gave gifts to men... And He gave the apostles, the prophets, the evangelists, the pastors and the teachers to equip the saints for the work of ministry for building up the body of Christ.'[27]

There are a number of observations here which apply to all the fivefold ministries. However, our focus is on prophets. So what can we see? Firstly, prophets are called by Jesus; Christ 'gave gifts to men'. There is a specific and individual call to the prophetic office which is not a general invitation, but a unique call. We can see this throughout the Old Testament as, like I mentioned before, many of the prophets had incredible life-changing encounters. Isaiah, Jeremiah and Ezekiel are just three to name. Clearly, prophets must be gifted in prophecy - and uniquely, powerfully so. There is an authority and endorsement that comes with a powerful prophetic gift. It doesn't negate character, of course, but godly and mature character

---

[26] Romans 15:4

[27] Ephesians 4:8, 11-12

accompanying a strong gift are signs of a prophet. If either is missing, we aren't talking about a prophet.

Secondly, it isn't just about the gift, but also who the man or woman is. The scripture says that, 'He (Christ) gave the... prophets... to the [church]. The *person* is the gift to the church, not just their abilities. There is something about who they are as an individual that is part of the package. Their personality, perceptions, insights and ways of thinking are just as much a part of the prophetic office as is their ability to prophesy. It is as much about who they are as it is about what they can do.

Thirdly, prophets are meant to 'equip the saints for the work of ministry'. Their role is to disciple, train and mentor believers in prophetic ministry. They reproduce themselves by helping others develop their own prophetic gifts. An authentic prophet is less concerned about being a superstar and more about helping others grow.

Fourthly, prophets have a heart to see the Church flourish because they want to be part of 'building up the body of Christ'. As such they are not only passionate about the church, but they are part of a church. As we've seen before, prophecy builds up, encourages and consoles people in community. Therefore a prophet understands that they must first be in a community to be able to do that, and so they also need to be in right relationship with the leaders of that community.

This means that prophets are not self-appointed; they live in community with other believers and over time, let their call, fruit and gift speak for themselves to a point whereby they are recognised by the members of that community and released to minister by the community leaders. It is an unhealthy sign for a prophet to not be part of a godly community, or be covered by godly leadership. If these things aren't present, it should raise red flags. Similarly, communities and leaders recognise their own prophets, as opposed to being told who their prophets are. Jesus taught that prophets reveal themselves by the fruit of their lives.[28] Community living and submission to leadership are the best revealers of fruit. It follows that an absence of either should be a concern. Calling ourselves 'prophet' doesn't necessarily mean we are! If you feel you have a call to the prophetic office, then get involved in community, serve your spiritual leaders, walk with God and become more like Him, and trust that He will increase your favour and influence in the right time, in the right way. Healthy prophets are a blessing to the church because they are foundational in the life of the local church,[29] so we need them!

Practising The Prophetic

We've seen that anyone and everyone, in the New Covenant, can hear God and speak as his representative prophetically. We've also learnt about prophets and characteristics of healthy prophets. These six attributes are godly character recognised by others, a strong prophetic gift endorsed by leaders and the community, a desire to disciple and train others in the prophetic ministry, a passion for the church, integration with a local community of believers, and wholehearted submission to spiritual leaders in that same community.

---

[28] Matthew 7:15-20

[29] Ephesians 2:20

Ask God, and other trusted people, including your church leader, how they feel you are progressing in each of these six areas and if there are any areas of concern they have. Listen to their opinions and take their advice. It'll help you grow.

PART II
PROPHETIC
STRUCTURE

I'm a big fan of football, although I had to reluctantly call it 'soccer' when I lived in the US. Over there, football is a very different thing that I don't really understand. Especially when they don't really use the foot, and definitely don't use a ball. But I understand why they didn't call the sport 'hand-egg'.

I played proper football to a fairly high level, which just means that sometimes I had access to heated changing rooms and pitches that had been cut and had the dogs mess removed before I went out on them. I wasn't good enough to be semi-professional and get paid to play though, which is when you've truly made it. I've heard legends that such players are guaranteed oranges at half-time.

The higher the level of sport you play, the more key the mental side becomes. Whilst the physical and technical aspects of the game were important, players had to have a certain level of tactical intelligence to understand what was happening during a match, and respond accordingly. It's fine having four pairs of lungs and bright rainbow boots that shower glitter as you do tricks, flicks and skills, but if you don't know basics of game management, positioning, reading a game, and tactical improvisation, you quickly become more of a burden than a blessing to the team. Less skilful players can actually be greater assets because of their aptitude and work ethic.

In all sports, and life in general, it seems a principle exists that natural talent can take you so far, but without diligence and training, the progress will halt. We have to train and hone our abilities. In the same way, if we want to grow in the area of prophecy, an increased understanding of the component parts of prophecy will help us sharpen our gift. In this section, I want to examine the structure of prophecy and see what it can teach us that will impact us positively as we continue to grow in our gift.

We can break down the essence of prophecy into three separate steps:

1. Revelation - what is God saying? How do we see, hear and sense it?
2. Interpretation - what does God mean? How can we understand what He says?
3. Application - what do we do now? How do we get the most out of His message?

In the forthcoming section, we will examine each of these. But before we do, let's examine the transmitters of prophecy - us.

4. Spiritual Mechanics

I quite like DIY, but I'm really bad at it. I'm convinced it isn't just practice, but that I'm flawed on a genetic level. All the men in my family, aside from me, are highly practical and know their way around a toolbox. My dad and all my brothers work in the building industry and have built impressive constructions, like, I don't know, house extensions. Real man things. Both my brothers-in-law excel at testosterone-fuelled construction. The only thing I can build is a spreadsheet. If I really want to show off, I'll include coloured cells and auto-filter features. I have a toolbox, but I don't think it's an impressive looking one because my daughter often mistakes it for one of her toy sets. Even my wife is better at DIY than me. She's a reconstructive surgeon and apparently, most of the tools used for carpentry are similar to instruments used in surgical procedures. Think that one through the next time you are going to the dentist. There is a saying that a bad workman blames his tools, but if my tools could speak I think they would blame me for some of the botch jobs I've attempted over the years. Still, I do think I've got better as I've practised. It now only takes me five attempts instead of six to put a screw in.

If that saying is true, does it also must mean that a good workman can take credit from his tools? To grow in prophecy, it helps to understand the tools involved. One of the tools used is us: humanity. So an understanding of how God created humans is helpful. The Apostle Paul tells the Corinthians that if he prays in tongues, his spirit prays, but his mind is unfruitful so he will pray with his mind as well.[30] Paul clearly distinguishes between two 'inner' parts of himself - his mind and his spirit - and says that they aren't always in alignment.

We all know we have an 'outer part', our body, which interacts with the visible, physical, material, 'seen' world. We also have an 'inner part' interacts with the invisible, spiritual, immaterial and 'unseen' world. The Bible uses different words to describe it which in English have been translated 'heart', 'spirit', and 'soul'. This 'inner man' incorporates our mind and emotions. So our mind, then, is the part of us that processes all the information we receive from our outer and inner parts. Humans aren't neatly compartmentalised so we can't say for sure where the spirit/soul is located, or where the mind stops and the spirit begins - if indeed, it really works like that. Thinking like this misses the point, which is that we are not just physical beings, but spiritual ones too. To be human means to value being flesh and blood just as much as we value being more than simple biological machines. Denial of either aspect dehumanises ourselves.

Understanding our humanity by valuing both our outer and inner lives helps us understand Apostle Paul's teaching in 1 Corinthians 2 and 3. In those chapters, he describes some of the different ways people live their lives.

Paul describes one group of people, whom he calls 'spiritual',[31] by using the word *pneumatikos*. *Pneuma* is the Greek word for spirit, and depending on the context can refer to the Holy Spirit, evil spirits, or the human spirit. A *pneumatikos* is a person who lives conscious

---

[30] 1 Corinthians 14:14-15

[31] 1 Corinthians 2:13

and connected to God, filled with the Spirit of God, indwelt and influenced by Him and able to correctly discern spiritual things. Biblically, being 'spiritual' is nothing to do with having special, secret knowledge. It is about being indwelt by God, living a life of obedience in response to His leading, and being transformed by Him.

Paul then refers to a second group of people who he calls 'natural'. He describes these people as not comprehending the things of the Spirit of God, instead interpreting those things as foolishness because they lack accurate spiritual discernment.[32] The word 'natural' is the Greek word *psuchikos*, which comes from the word *psuche*. It is the foundation for our English word 'psychology'. The concept of *psuche* is that of the human 'life-force' and is often translated 'soul'. In effect, it is the immaterial thing that makes us human. On its own, it is neither a positive nor a negative word. But in this passage, because Paul is contrasting it with *pneumatikos,* being a *psuchikos* is not a good thing. The life of a *psuchikos* is dictated primarily by the passions of their soul; they look to satisfy their appetites and desires. To Paul, this is the way non-Christians, by nature, live, because they are humans not infilled with and led by the Spirit of God.

Later, Paul tells the Corinthians about a third group of people who he says are 'of the flesh'.[33] Whenever Paul talks about 'the flesh', he contrasts it with the spirit to illustrate the difference between living a worldly life and living a godly life. This is the case in these verses because Paul is rebuking some of the Corinthians for living life in the flesh as they embrace jealousy, strife and divisiveness. Paul isn't

---

[32] 1 Corinthians 2:14

[33] 1 Corinthians 3:1-4

writing to non-believers here though. He is writing to the prophesying, miracle-working, Jesus-believing Corinthian church. This tells us that even as Christians, we can live from a place of power and influence of the Holy Spirit, or from the flesh - we could use the phrase 'carnal Christians' to describe them. We all know carnal Christians. They are the people we know who believe but have a very different lifestyle going on. They might be backsliders or prodigals. But more soberly, we might be carnal. We might live from a carnal place one week, or one day, or one hour, or one moment when we let our unsanctified human instincts or passions drive us, instead of yielding to God's leading.

Paul talks a lot about this in the letters to the Romans and Galatians. Christians can live as *pneumatikos* - Spirit-led - or we can live life as if we were *psuchikos,* even though that is not our identity now that we are new creations in Christ'.[34] The 'flesh' is Paul's way of talking about our old, before Christ, 'natural' ways of living, feeling and acting - led by our ungodly passions, with all its self-indulgent drives and appetites being the centre of how we live our lives. Whenever we give in to temptation, we are indulging the flesh. As Christians, we have a choice - do we live 'naturally', or live by the leading of the Spirit?

Why does this matter when talking about prophecy? The answer is because we want to prophesy with revelation we receive in our spirit and not from our flesh, so it is important that we are able to discern the difference. This introduces us to the concept of revelation, which we will look at in the next chapter.

---

[34] 2 Corinthians 5:17

Practising The Prophetic

We've seen that as people, we are made up of two parts - our outer and inner part. As Christians, we can choose to live two ways - led by the Spirit, because we are indwelt by God's Spirit, or led by the flesh, meaning a self-satisfying and me-centred lifestyle. Spend some time with God and ask Him if there are any areas in your life that remain 'fleshly'. If He puts his finger on anything, confess it and repent, making a plan of what you are going to do in response to show your repentance is a genuine one that leads to spiritual fruit.

5. Finding the Right Frequency

Sometimes I want to mix things up a little, and instead of listening to my streamed or downloaded music, I will listen to the radio. Some radio stations I like are broadcast nationally. Once I find the right frequency I can get a clear signal and can listen without any disruption. Other stations are regional or even local, so have a smaller broadcasting area. This means that if I moved out of their zone, the previously clear signal begins to diminish in quality to the point where it can be unlistenable, fuzzing with static. Driving presents interesting challenges, especially if I am driving to a different region. A frequency previously clear for one station can change to be a mixture of two stations, competing for my attention. Hearing different voices or songs can be annoying. A quirky occurrence is when one of those stations isn't English. Growing up in the south of England, it can be quite confusing when your perfectly tuned radio stops playing indie rock and begins churning out distorted French operetta or German rap. Finding the right frequency as the source is essential to hearing clearly.

The word 'revelation' simply means 'revealing'. There is a sense of unveiling or disclosing with it. It is why the last book of the Bible is called Revelation - it is about the final unveiling of Jesus Christ, when all will see Him for who He truly is. But revelation is also key to us as Christians because God speaks to us and reveals things - revelations. The Apostle Paul tells the Corinthians:

'So also no one comprehends the thoughts of God except the Spirit of God. Now we have received not the spirit of the world, but the Spirit who is from God, that we might understand the things freely given us by God. And we impart this in words not taught by human wisdom but taught by the Spirit interpreting spiritual truths to those who are spiritual.' [35]

The Spirit of God, who knows the thoughts of God, makes His home in us. Because God is spirit,[36] meaning immaterial, He teaches us spiritual truths by speaking to our spirits. Therefore revelation from God is always Spirit to spirit communication - God's Spirit speaking to our spirit. The process of revelation could get messy if there is an issue with God's Spirit (which isn't going to happen), an issue with our spirit, or interference with the connection between the two.

As we learnt in the previous chapter, we are spiritual creatures because we have a spirit. Our spirits can interact with the spiritual realm, which is why we can sense God's presence. Christians and non-Christians alike can sense in the spirit realm, which means they can sense God. Some people have taught that non-Christians can't sense God because they are 'spiritually dead', but this is incorrect. Biblically, spiritual death doesn't mean that someone doesn't have a spirit - after all, to be human is to have a spirit. It means there is no permanent connection to God. That's why Jesus said he came to bring life[37] - meaning, spiritual connection to God.

---

[35] 1 Corinthians 2:11-13

[36] John 4:24

[37] John 10:10

God is not the only being present in the spiritual realm. Other beings dwell there, such as angels and demons. Angels and demons can both be sources of revelation, examples of which we see throughout scripture. There are many accounts of God's people conversing with angels, and the book of Acts tells us about a slave-girl in Philippi who is demonized with a spirit of divination - a demonic being indwelling insider her that gave her a counterfeit gift of prophecy. Paul sets her free from the demonic influence, much to the anger of her owners who we no doubt making a tidy profit from her 'prophecies'.[38] This account shows that we can receive revelation from sources other than God. This explains the existence of the Occult, for example. 'Occult' means 'hidden', which is interesting considering we're talking about revelation, which reveals the hidden. I don't believe that all occultic practices are trickery. Sure, some may well be, but others will be genuine. The issue isn't the accuracy, but the source. Accurate divination from an ungodly source will, ultimately, only build up, encourage, or comfort in the short-term. In the long-term, what agenda, deception or influence will be gaining momentum under the surface?

As well as the Lord, angels and demons, strangely enough, we can also be a source of revelation! This is often called 'soulish' prophecy because the revelations are not from the Spirit of God but from ourselves. On one level, this may well be a simple mistake and something we aren't conscious of, but there may be occasions when people do this deliberately, using information obtained through observation, intuition, cold-reading or even deception and clothing it as 'prophecy' to speak out something previously unknown. With sincere believers eagerly desiring to prophesy (which is always a good thing), it is entirely possible that we simply get it wrong and

[38] Acts 16:16-19

instead of prophesying from the Spirit - God's thoughts and feelings - we prophesy from our self - our thoughts and feelings. It's important to understand that just because gets it wrong once or twice, it doesn't automatically mean they have constant soulish prophetic revelations or trying to deceive. Let's put the 'false prophet' accusations down for one moment and back away slowly. The Bible talks about this, using a term to show that in effect, all of us, when we prophesy, really speak out with a mixture of spiritual and soulish prophecy. The Bible calls this 'prophesying in part'.[39] It would follow that prophetic maturity is simply the journey of us decreasing the amount of soulish prophecy we do whilst increasingly prophesying from our spirit as we truly hear from God.

Practising The Prophetic

Consider how you personally engage with God's presence. How do you draw near to Him? Is there anything that you notice helps you connect with God? Prayer? Worship? Scripture? Walking in creation? If you aren't sure, experiment with different things over the next few days and see what keys God has given you to help you 'practise His presence.' If/when you know how to best connect with God, spend some time planning how you can best do it in a new way that you haven't done before. Perhaps earlier. Perhaps later. Perhaps longer. Perhaps more consistently. Whatever it is, commit yourself to your plan and see how it impacts your walk with God in the next few days.

---

[39] 1 Corinthians 13:9

6. Holy Writ

I didn't grow up in a Christian family so when I started attending church, Bibles seemed a funny thing to me. I also observed that Christians in this new happy-clappy church I was going to had some secret code that demonstrated their holiness, with the Bible being the key to understanding this system. For example, the heavy hitters all had leather or faux-leather bound Bibles whilst the amateurs had hardback or even paperback bibles. Also, the bigger the Bible, the better Christian they seemed to be. It seemed to be a good thing to own a Bible so heavy that it needed its own set of wheels. The superstars had Bibles that not only had the normal million pages the Bible came with anyway, but also uncountable appendices of maps, illustrations, study notes, concordances, and ancient Hebrew recipes. Then, there were the bookmarks. Using a place marker said 'I'm a serious reader', but the A-team had bookmarks with a myriad of coloured ribbons on. These legends not only read the Bible but read multiple sections **at the same time**. Imagine what anyone would think about me if they learnt I marked my page by folding down the corner. The final coup de grace was the badge of honour - a sticker of a little fish sign on the front covers. You know the one. Yet only the wives of the church leaders could have these symbols of status. I truly wondered if I would ever get to Heaven when I looked at my paperback, cola-stained, illustrated children's Bible.

The Bible is important in the life of the believer. One of the main ways God speaks to us is through the Bible. In fact, prophetic maturity will not happen outside of a knowledge and familiarity with the scriptures. There is a fascinating dialogue in Mark 12 between Jesus and the Sadducees. The Sadducees don't believe in an afterlife, and so concoct a quite incredible situation involving a woman marrying seven men, each of whom dies, and present Jesus with a theological question they hope will stump Him. Putting aside the suspicions many of us would have if we truly knew someone who had seven of their husbands die in 'mysterious' circumstances, Jesus answers their question, and at the same time challenges them both in their knowledge of God and understanding of the scriptures.[40] He says to them, quite bluntly, that "you [Sadducees] are wrong, because you know neither the Scriptures nor the power of God."

There is a unique partnership between the scriptures and the Holy Spirit that is vital for our spiritual maturity - we need to know and experience both. God loves to bring revelation through the scriptures, while knowledge of the scriptures will both fuel and guide our revelations and encounters.

In Luke 24, two of Jesus' disciples are walking on the Emmaus road. Jesus - who they fail to recognise - joins them on their pilgrimage and walks with them. As the conversation moves to spiritual things, Jesus masterfully takes them on a journey through the Old Testament, explaining how everything in it points to Him. After He leaves, the disciples look at each other and say, "didn't our hearts burn within us while He opened up the scriptures?"[41] Holy Spirit stirred inside them as Jesus spoke to them through the scriptures, making the pages, words and stories come alive. Theologians call this phenomena 'illumination' - when light is shed upon the

[40] Mark 12:24-27

[41] Luke 24:32

scriptures and they become clear to us. For that to happen, we need to read the Bible ourselves and let God speak to us through it.

The Greek word *graphe* is the word used in the New Testament when discussing the written scriptures. When Paul wrote his first letter to his student Timothy, he told him 'all scripture (*graphe*) is breathed out by God and profitable for teaching, for reproof, for correction, and for training in righteousness, that the man of God may be complete, equipped for every good work.'[42] The Greek word translated 'breathed out by God' is *theopneustos.* Some other translations translate this word into 'inspired'. We're familiar with the idea of inspiration, using it to communicate the idea of something being exceptional - it is 'inspired' - or something can lift our spirits - it is 'inspiring'. But neither of these meanings capture the essence of what Paul is trying to convey to Timothy in using *theopneustos*. Paul is wanting Timothy to understand that the biblical writings are more than just historical accounts or stories about God. He has inspired - originated them. The Bible comes to us through men but from God. Just as when we speak, we breathe, God's words were carried to the human authors by his Spirit, his *pneuma* - the Greek word for both breath and spirit. The writings contained within originate from the heart and mind of God, and so are of infinite value and benefit to us.

One time, I was counselling a man who considered himself to be very prophetic. He was sharing what He felt God was saying to Him but I had an unease about some of the things He was sharing. They all sounded wonderfully spiritual, profound and deep, but fundamentally, the message was contrary to elements of scripture.

---

[42] 2 Timothy 3:15-17

When I shared this with him, his response was "I'm not a word guy, I'm more of a Spirit man." The implication was that he didn't know the Bible that well, but that was OK because God spoke to him in other ways. The only problem was that his message from God didn't sound like it lined up with things God had already said!

A true understanding of scripture as being inspired and God-breathed helps us avoid some of the errors that can creep in when we are navigating the relationship between the Bible and the prophetic.

Firstly, if scripture is God-Breathed then it must have **authority**. Its words have weight and should shape our thinking. If we and the scriptures are in disagreement, we should be the ones who move!

Secondly, if scripture is God-breathed then it must be **revelatory**. Not only because the words contained within are revelations from God that should be prized, but because Holy Spirit will continually remind, refresh and re-present timeless scriptural truths to us to help us get to know God more deeply.

Thirdly, if scripture is God-Breathed then it must be **accessible**. Why would God give us something of such value and make it impossible to understand? Yes, there are difficult passages but oftentimes if we cultivate the diligent study of historical and cultural contexts, read good commentaries, develop an understanding of the big picture of the Bible, and have the humility to ask questions, we will learn and therefore grow.

Fourthly, if scripture is God-Breathed then it must be **necessary.** No words contained within it are wasted or pointless. Whilst the life and words of Jesus function as our primary lens to understand much of the rest of the scriptures, that doesn't relegate other writings to irrelevancy. It all reveals something of the heart of God, and He doesn't waste words.

Prophetically, when we read the scriptures and God speaks to us, the purpose is not simply stimulation but is transformation. Revelation should lead to realization, then repentance, which in turn takes us towards transformation. The Bible is a catalyst for encounters with God. It isn't the encounter itself but directs us to its Author as we are impacted by its words. This is why academic study without genuine Holy Spirit interaction is dangerous. The goal should never be education, but transformation. Interestingly, some Christians can accuse others of being full of head knowledge, dryness and academia whilst having their own blind spots as they spend time overly studying the end times, spiritual warfare, demonology, numerology, the Nephilim, and other favourite niche subjects. We all can gravitate towards our own extremes. I value systematic theology highly. Learning what the Bible teaches about specific subjects was invaluable for me. But I was equally impacted by biblical theology, seeing how the story of God unfolded and progressed as the Bible was written. We need both.

The Bible creates a hunger for itself as it is read by believers. There are a number of practices that can help us prepare ourselves for encounter through the written word.

Firstly, *regular reading*. Whether this takes the form of daily study notes or a reading plan, learn what works for you. Daily is certainly recommended. Connecting bible reading to worship and encounter through practices such as *Lectio Divina*[43] will help some people, especially those who are prophetic.

Secondly, *regular review*. Reviewing and journaling what you have been reading is incredibly beneficial. The nature and frequency of this can take different forms, but a way of engaging and processing with the text can help cement what God is saying to you.

Thirdly, *regular study*. Whether this is formal or informal, beginner or advanced, individual or corporate, learning from teachers and preachers cannot help but be advantageous. I would encourage studying doctrine and theology in both systematic and biblical forms. This ensures a balance in learning not only how the Bible unfolds and develops thematically, but also what it says specifically about certain topics.

Fourthly, *regular response*. James tells us to not just be hearers of the word, but doers as well.[44] Information without application prevents transformation. Change is the goal of engaging with Scripture.

The Bible is essential for healthy, spiritual growth. It is, by nature, prophetic, because it reveals the heart and mind of God. Healthy prophetic growth cannot happen outside of deepening our passion for the scriptures. We're to be a people of the book because we understand the book is also a gateway.

---

[43] http://en.wikipedia.org/wiki/Lectio_divina

[44] James 1:22

Practising The Prophetic

Get alone with God and your Bible, at a quiet and undisturbed time if possible. Still yourself before God, find your favourite Psalm, and read the written word with the Living Word using the following process:

- **Read** - *Read slowly. Read out loud, listening to yourself say the words. Repeat the verses and place the emphasis on different words in sentences.*

- **Reflect** - *What stands out? What are you drawn to? What words, phrases or illustrations? Chew it over in your mind - this is what Biblical Meditation is. Don't over-think; just keep reading until something stands out. When it does, linger. Don't be too quick to move on. God is speaking!*

- **Respond** - *Start to thank God for what He's saying. Tell him what you know about what He is telling you. What does it mean to you? What does it tell you about Him? How does it affect your feelings or your life? Use it as a catalyst to prayerful dialogue with God in your heart or even out loud. Then turn into worship!*

- **Rest** - *When you sense the presence of God, rest. Linger. Enjoy Him!*

7. Heavenly Spectacles

I really dislike sunglasses. To be honest, I dislike the sun and so anything associated with hot weather automatically goes on my 'dislike list', which is probably too long and says a lot about me. I dislike beaches because the sand gets everywhere. I dislike heat because then I sweat and feel unclean. I dislike sun cream because then my skin feels like a bizarre ooze of creamy sweat cream. I dislike swimming because swimming pools seem to be giant collections of other peoples used bathwater. You may be utterly unsurprised at my dislike for sunglasses. I find them uncomfortable, and frustrating. I'm led to believe that sunglasses are actually intended to help vision in the sunshine, and not merely help cool-looking people look even cooler whilst making me feel like I fell out of the unfashionable tree and hit every branch on the way down. Instead, I find sunglasses are either too light, which lets in all the light and so blinds me, or too dark, which blocks out all the light and so blinds me. So I seem to only have two choices: blindness induced by inept sunglasses or blindness induced by a vengeful sun. Either way, what and how I see is going to be impacted.

Sometimes, God wants to influence what and how we see because He has something to say to us. In fact, it seems to be one of the primary ways He speaks to those that He loves. With this in mind, this and the next chapter will look at some of the ways God speaks to us through our physical or spiritual eyes.

Visions and Trances

Visions are simply images, which can be either still or be moving, that we 'see'. There are two types of vision - a vision of the mind, and an open vision.

A vision of the mind would be seen in our 'mind's eye'. An example would be when people prophesy and say "I see a picture of…" and are very common. During the worship time of a church meeting I attended, I saw a large, shaven-headed, muscular, scary looking gentleman the other side of the room. As I looked at him, I saw a picture of him running during the night, wearing an orange jumpsuit, with a prison in the background and a police helicopter searching for him using a spotlight. The sense was that God was saying that this gentleman was running away from Him, trying to escape, but God was pursuing him because He loved him and wanted a relationship. I walked over to the man and spoke to him, which makes it all sound incredibly easy, but in reality took a lot longer than it should have because all I could see in my mind now was a vision of this large, muscular man crushing me for sharing such a bizarre picture. Anyway, once I obeyed God and not my self-preservation instinct, the man listened to me share this picture with him (the first picture, not the one where he crushes me). He went on to tell me that he had only just been released from prison and this was the first time he had come to church. He came from a Christian family and was now trying to put his life right before God and people. My picture had encouraged him that God was for him, and not against him.

An open vision is similar to a vision of the mind, but instead of seeing images and pictures with our spiritual eyes, we see them with our physical eyes. These are less common and can resemble an image being 'overlaid' on top of what is right in front of us.

Sometimes when I'm ministering to someone, I will see a word or picture 'written' or superimposed over their head. I remember praying with a gentleman and seeing superimposed on his chest a picture of a Native American wigwam. There was a sense that he was a spiritual man but hadn't found a permanent 'home', so had been spiritually wandering. Sharing it with him opened up a conversation about finding a local church, committing to it and investing in it as a 'home'.

Someone who sees visions, whatever type, is seeing in the Spirit and can be called a 'seer'. There is some teaching floating around that seers have unusual anointings and so are to be considered as super-prophets because they see into the spirit realm. Some seers may have a high level of spiritual sight, and see things many people do not. But spiritual sight is common amongst God's prophetic people, so the term 'seer' is less of a title and more of a description of how some people receive revelation from the Lord. In the Old Testament, the writer of 1 Samuel tells us that, *'formerly in Israel, when a man went to inquire of God, he said, "Come, let us go to the seer," for today's 'prophet' was formerly called a seer.'* [45] It seems that for the people of Israel, whilst at one point they distinguished between prophets and seers, by the time of King Saul approximately a thousand years before Christ, the two terms were absorbed under the term 'prophet'. 'Seer' was used to identify a chosen servant of God, to whom He spoke visually. Ultimately, if you are a seer, that is great, whatever the level of your seeing. If you aren't, that is fine as well. Rather than obtaining our identity from a title that the Bible doesn't give in the New Testament, let's be more excited about the fact God is speaking to us to be a blessing to others. Let's not fixate

---

[45] 1 Samuel 9:9

on the transmission method of Spirit to spirit; the message is most important, not the method by which it is received.

A trance is when, in the Spirit, we 'zone out' of where we are and become more aware of the spiritual realm. It is not a physical translocation, but a heightened awareness. During a trance, God will speak to us, often by presenting things before our eyes. Peter has a trance in Acts 10:9-11 where God reveals to him the acceptance of the Gentiles in the New Covenant. The Greek word for trance is *ekstasis,* from which we get the English word 'ecstasy', which is both an intense emotion of delight and a drug that causes people to have extreme psychological experiences. This fits in with the definition of the Greek word, which can mean 'out of your mind'. A trance, then, is a feeling of being out of our mind - unaware of where we are or what we were doing - and God speaks to us.

Angels

Another way we see in the Spirit is through Angels. Again, this can be seeing with our physical eyes or our mind's eyes. I've seen angels a handful of times, mostly in my mind's eye, but not always. The writer of Hebrews tells us that angels are spirits whose role is to serve those who are meant to inherit salvation.[46] The Greek word for angel is *angelos,* which means 'messenger'. This gives an insight into their function: they communicate messages to us, and in my experience, this might be a verbal message or it might be non-verbal.

On one occasion, I was having a very significant - eternally significant - conversation with someone close to me about a subject that historically, had caused issues between us. I was nervous about proceeding deeper into the issue because my experience had been

[46] Hebrews 1:13-14

that no matter how gentle or polite I was, this individual became evasive and threw up proverbial walls. I didn't want that to happen but wasn't sure how to proceed. I prayed and asked God for wisdom, then saw movement out of the corner of my left eye. I turned and saw an angel - well, it was either an angel or a strange man dressed in some very interesting clothing, had just walked into my house! As my brain caught up with my eyes, the angel smiled at me and gave me a 'thumbs up' symbol, which I took to mean I could continue this conversation, free from anxiety and concern. It ended up being an incredible conversation which, funnily enough, ended up being more ministry for me than the other party, despite my original expectations!

Simply put, if you see an angel, whether with your mind's eye or natural eyes, ask it what its message is. Scripture has a number of human to angel conversations, and whether the response is audible or not, the angel is simply doing its job in ministering to you. Conversing with an angel is not the same as worshipping it. In one ministry meeting I was in, the preacher was talking about healing and I saw in my spirit an angel on the right of the stage, looking at me. I asked it what it was doing here - because scripturally, angels always have a purpose or job - and it told me it was there for healing. That moment, I got a download of half a dozen or so physical conditions, which I interpreted as words of knowledge. Sure enough, as I shared them later, people responded and a number of people were healed of those and other afflictions.

Some people seem to have angelic conversations or announcements every half-hour, or daily visitations as they are just about to go shopping for groceries, but whether those are accurate or not, the same principle applies here as to any seeing in the spirit we may do.

It is less about the method of transmission and more about the message. Angelic encounters are not a measure of spirituality, but they do seem to be involved in adding gravitas and credibility to something God says. Scripturally, angelic announcements carry a lot of weight. My current working theory is the more God wants you to pay attention to something, the more unusually He speaks it. This may include the angelic messenger. But it is a working theory, so ask me again in ten years' time!

Practising The Prophetic

If we want God to show us things to see, it's a good idea to consecrate our eyes to Him. Take some time to speak with Him and see if there is anything you currently watch or look at that He wants to discuss with you - for example, certain movies, TV shows, pornography. Then repent. Whether there is something or not, place your hands on your eyes and pray a prayer of dedication that your eyes belong to Him, and ask Him to open your eyes to see all that He wants you to see. Expect to see new things with your natural and spiritual eyes!

8. Works Like a Dream

Dreams are sequences of images, ideas, emotions and sensations that occur involuntarily during sleep. Some of the earliest scriptural accounts of seeing in the Spirit come in the forms of dreams. Abraham, Jacob and Joseph all have dreams through which God speaks to them. The twin themes of dreams and dream interpretation are littered throughout scripture, in both Old and New Testaments. There is an interesting passage in Job which gives us some clues as to the purpose of 'God-dreams':

'For God speaks in one way, and in two, though man does not perceive it. In a dream, in a vision of the night, when deep sleep falls on men, while they slumber on their beds, then He opens the ears of men and terrifies them with warnings, that He may turn aside from his deed and conceal pride from a man.' [47]

This passage suggests that God gives us dreams for a number of reasons. The first might be when we wouldn't otherwise be responsive to the message if we heard it through more established means. When I was a new convert, an older gentleman in his forties - which is ancient when you are a teenager - came to me with some advice about a hobby of mine that he felt wasn't helpful for me as a young believer. It wasn't a sinful, illegal or immoral activity and I couldn't find any explicit or implicit objection to it biblically. Being fifteen and knowing everything in the world, or more accurately *thinking* I knew everything, I asked him to show me in the Bible

---

[47] Job 33:14-18

where it said that my preferred pastime wasn't on God's approval list. I wasn't being argumentative, rebellious or unteachable; I just had a high value for truth and didn't want to be bound by someone else's interpretations, conscience or standards. That night, I had a dream, my first 'God-dream', where I saw a bookcase filled with books of different colours and thicknesses. Each book had writing on the spine that corresponded to a different area of my life. Suddenly a hand appeared, which I knew was the hand of God, and starting scanning across the bookcase, stopping to take out certain books from the bookcase and place them in a pile. One of the removed books had the aforementioned hobby on the spine. When I awoke, I knew that God was telling me that this activity had no place in my life. I didn't need any further convincing; God had spoken to my spirit and that was enough. This illustrates the first category of dreams: speaking to our inner man when other means of communication maybe aren't quite getting through.

Secondly, dreams can be warnings. Once, I was on the verge of making a significant life decision and considering what I should do. It looked good on the surface and wise, godly people were affirming that I embrace the opportunity. God gave me a dream whereby I saw myself wearing clothing connected to the potential decision. In the dream, the clothing was far too big for me, looking untidy and feeling uncomfortable. The people who would have been involved in this life decision with me were also present in the dream but were walking together on the other side of a river, in the opposite direction to me. I woke knowing that I the opportunity in front of me wouldn't be a 'good fit'. Plus, the people who were advising me and I would be involved with were going in a different direction in life to where I was heading. This warning helped me make a good decision and decline the opportunity.

Thirdly, dreams can bring direction change. The book of Acts tells us that the Apostle Paul was planning his itinerant ministry tour, and had a 'vision of the night' where he saw someone from Macedonia pleading with him to come to them. This, subsequently, caused a change of plans.[48] A 'vision of the night' sounds a lot like a dream to me!

It's worth stating that not every dream is from the spirit realm. Scripture tells us that some come from our mind. The author of Ecclesiastes tells us that *the dream comes with much business.*[49] The Hebrew word for 'business' can mean job, task, occupation, work or venture. If we have lots of busyness going on and things on our mind, perhaps even stress, we shouldn't be surprised if we have dreams.

If not all dreams come from the spirit realm, then the ability to have dreams in and of themselves isn't prophetic. Interpreting a 'God dream' and making sense of the meaning behind it is the prophetic aspect. Dreams are often full of symbols, numbers and colours and God's first language isn't necessarily ours. Prayer is key to unlocking the meaning of a dream - or even discerning whether it is a God dream or not. There are many books written which have much wisdom on the subject of interpreting dreams. Some would suggest that different colours, symbols or numbers have symbolic interpretations. Whilst there is some truth in that, I would propose that God's heart is for us to seek Him for the meaning and not rely solely on a manual. I heard a well-known and respected prophet tell the story that a prophetic group he led was beginning to seek God for

[48] Acts 16:9-10

[49] Ecclesiastes 5:3

dream interpretations, and had people in the church come to them with dreams they desired to understand. His team prayed and sought the Lord, who gave them insight which they could relay back to astounded and encouraged individuals. This happened more and more frequently, and the team became aware of a real grace in this area of dream interpretation. Then a well-meaning member of the team introduced a dream interpretation manual, which was written like an encyclopedia with alphabetical references to various animals, buildings, people, symbols or colours that could appear in dreams. This manual began to become the 'go to' for the team members as they sought interpretations, but over time the team noticed that their accuracy was declining, and the success and grace they had previously experienced seemed to lift. They repented and returned to what they originally did, and began to see accuracy return.

I'm not dismissing these helpful tools, but I would caution us to remember what they are: tools. Courses and books are never meant to replace the intimacy of seeking the Dream Giver for the meaning of the dream. Dreams are worth writing down, praying over, sharing with prophetic friends, and, yes, looking at reputable resources for guidance. Let Holy Spirit speak through any and all of these to see what God is saying to you through your dreams - or someone else's, if you are looking to develop your dream interpretation.

Practising The Prophetic

If you want God to speak to you through your dreams, then sleeping helps! Take some time to do a 'sleep review' to see if there are any steps you can take to improve the overall quality of your sleep. Whether you have changes to make or not, dedicate your sleep to God and ask Him to give you dreams. Keep something to write with close by your bed, so when you wake up and a dream is fresh in your memory, you can write it down to remember and review later. Pray about any dreams God gives you and seek Him for interpretations. What emotions, images, people or situations stand out? Ask God for insight on them. As you grow in confidence, ask God to give you opportunities to interpret the dreams of other people. Following the same steps of prayer, seek God for an interpretation and share it!

9. God Whispers

Genuinely talented musicians fascinate me. Probably because I'm clearly not one. My one public performance didn't go very well. I was a schoolchild, probably eleven or twelve years old, and part of an orchestra. Of course, it wasn't a proper orchestra. Proper orchestras have instruments that cost serious money, and talented people who can play them properly and not simply use them as hitting or shooting utensils. No, this orchestra was for the peasants so we had instruments like triangles, wood blocks, scrapers (surely not the official name), and for the star performer, a glockenspiel. A glockenspiel was like a xylophone made by Fisher Price, and to prevent the bashers (you know, the things you hit it with to make sounds) becoming weapons, they had what looked and felt like giant cotton buds on the end. The teacher would say we were a 'percussion band' but all I wanted to know was why I wasn't allowed to use a trumpet, which would be loud and fun, or a violin, which I was convinced I could turn into a bow and arrow type weapon. Anyway, we had this recital of Silent Night to perform. I say perform, but there was no audience. We couldn't be trusted to play anything of any quality in public. So the poor music teacher had to endure multiple repeat performances of mistimed aural forms of anarchy. Much like a jazz concert. My role was simple. I had one job - to hit my triangle not too soft, not too hard, right at the end. Surprisingly, this seemed too hard for me to do, and many a 'performance' was ruined with me hitting too early, too late, too hard, too soft or a combination of these four variables. Yet to me, all my efforts sounded the same, which was pitch perfect, and the rest of the orchestra was in error. I was surprised when I wasn't invited back to join the next orchestra, which was renamed the 'music group'. But it was their loss. I understood that my classmates had misunderstood my talent, all because they couldn't hear what I hear.

Because God is a God who speaks, we should be a people who listen. As well as speaking through symbols and imagery, He also speaks to us in words, phrases and sentences. Similar to seeing in the spirit, we can hear in the spirit. Again, this could be with our spiritual ears or our physical ears. The account of the Tower of Babel[50] tells us that all languages originate from Him. Being sovereign and all-knowing, He can speak to us using all of them, or speak to us without using words. God's first language isn't necessarily English! Fortunately, God understands that effective communication only happens when the recipient of the communication can understand it. So what are the ways we can hear God?

God's Still, Small Voice

Throughout scripture, the phrase 'word of the Lord' appears over 250 times. In the New Testament it refers to the message of the Gospel but the majority of the references occur in the Old Testament. This phrase is often used to describe a prophet receiving some kind of revelation from God. God speaks to him and the prophet describes it as 'the word of the Lord came to me', or something similar. One example would be Elijah in 1 Kings 19, whereby he hides in a cave on Mount Horeb and the word of the Lord comes to him.[51] The story goes on to teach that God speaks through whispers at times and

[50] Genesis 11:1-9

[51] 1 Kings 19:9

not necessarily always extreme ways or means. We can only hear whispers when we are close to the whisperer, with our ears inclined to his mouth. It is a beautiful picture of intimacy and focus because we have to focus on the Whisperer to discern what He is saying. The still, small voice, then, tells us that we need to be still, and learn to shut out distractions because God's voice can be small - not because of impotence, but because He desires to draw us close to Him in intimacy and connection. This must be why the Psalmist says, 'be still and know that I am God.'[52]

Practically, this 'hearing' can take the form of a passing thought, word, phrase or sentence. Sometimes it is a scripture or part of a scripture. It could be a word of knowledge. I've even heard song lyrics! For me, they take the form of word clues that help me ask a good question, discern something about a situation, or show me something I need to pay attention to. Additionally, God will speak scriptures to me when I'm counselling someone, to help steer our conversation. It is a quiet, peaceful, gentle voice in my spirit that doesn't sound like me, and I'm totally able to ignore - but in my experience, it's better to listen to! On one occasion, I was ministering to a married couple and when I looked at the wife, I heard in my spirit the phrase 'refuge centre'. It opened up a line of conversation and ministry because one of her dreams that currently was on the back shelf was to open a centre to protect victims of sex trafficking.

This way of God speaking seems very common amongst His people, probably because it is by nature a very intimate and beautiful thing. I like to think of it as the sharing of the secrets of Heaven. We share our secrets with those that we love, and when they love us in return,

---

[52] Psalm 46:10

we don't need to shout, scream or holler to get their undivided attention.

Sounds In The Spirit Realm

It is entirely possible for God to speak through sounds, noises and songs as well as words. Similar, in a way, to visual clues, sounds in the Spirit are symbolic and require interpretation and understanding. For example, when I was once ministering to a gentleman, God gave me a prophetic word for Him which came to me by the way of the sound of a huge lock opening as a key turned, followed by other keys turning and locks opening. I didn't see anything but could hear this cascading effect in the unseen realm. I knew it to mean a new season of opportunity was opening up, so I shared this with him, which encouraged him and he confirmed that this was something he was feeling God speaking to him about personally.

The Audible Voice of God

Another possible way of hearing God is if He speaks audibly and directly. This doesn't seem as common as some of the other ways, but I have met people who have heard God speak to them this way. It is certainly apparent through scripture when God calls some of the Old Testament heroes to the prophetic ministry, He directly addresses them. Scripturally, it seems to be a pattern that God speaks audibly when He wants to communicate with someone something incredibly unexpected or destiny-shaping, to further His purposes. For example, the calling of Samuel, who would be the last Judge of Israel and the prophet who God used to usher in the kingship. Scripturally, God also seems to audibly speak when an event takes place that is epoch-shaping, such as Jesus' baptism[53] or his

---

53 Luke 3:22

Transfiguration[54]. It is almost as if God speaks audibly to create a line in the sand to indicate a significant shift in the life or lives of the hearers. Basically, something big is happening! It is also interesting to see that even when God spoke audibly, not everyone heard and mistook it for thunder[55]. Spiritual deafness can reach profound levels.

One beautiful story I heard regarding the audible voice of the Lord was of a gentleman who was in a nation fiercely closed to Christianity, the Gospel, and in which Christians, especially converts, are actively ostracised and persecuted. He was a spiritual leader of the national religion of that nation, and one day was alone in his house when he heard an audible voice tell him "you are a sheep amongst wolves." He described the voice as being both incredibly loving and yet incredibly powerful at the same time, and was scared, especially when he searched his house and could not find anyone present. He continued and the voice spoke again, repeating the phrase. In a contemporary echo to the aforementioned calling of Samuel, this gentlemen responded to the voice and asked: "who are you and what do you mean?". That night, he had a dream where a figure in white appeared to him and who explained to the man what He meant. The man realised that this figure in white was Jesus and understandably, converted soon after!

---

[54] Matt 17:5

[55] John 12:28-29

Practising The Prophetic

If we want God to say things to us to hear, it's a good idea to consecrate our ears to Him. Take some time to speak with Him and see if there is anything you currently listen to that He wants to discuss with you - for example, certain music, media or types of conversation. Then repent. Whether there is something or not, place your hands on your ears and pray a prayer of dedication that your ears belong to Him, and ask Him to open your ears to hear all that He wants you to hear. Expect to hear new things with your natural and spiritual ears!

10. Sense & Sensitivity

I have to confess, I love the internet. I have everything in the Cloud. Even this book started life as a Google Doc, meaning it autosaved every nanosecond. Let's just say I've had one too many documents fatally and irretrievably crash on me just before deadlines were due. One of the things I like the most about the web is that almost anything can be accessed on multiple devices and downloaded if need be. Films, TV shows, music, books, calendars, task lists, bank accounts, utility bills... the list goes on. All you need is a WiFi connection, which are plentiful once you agree to sign up to some email list which is impossible to unsubscribe from despite a big red button saying so, which will then go on to try to sell you irrelevant products by bombarding your inbox with seizure-inducing flashing messages every three minutes.

Getting revelation from God is like getting a spiritual download. Depending on the connection or bandwidth, the download might be rapid, slow or incomplete. It might come in stages. In the same way we have a physical sense of touch that interacts with the world around us, we have a spiritual sense of touch which interacts with the unseen world. So how do we sense God?

Impressions

An impression is when you experience unexpected emotions, feelings or convictions in a certain place, in a certain moment or around a certain person. It can be a real emotion, a sense of what God is feeling about something, or perhaps it manifests as a sense in your gut or even a mental insight like having an epiphany or a 'lightbulb moment'. You just know something because you know something, even without any kind of evidence or corroboration. You just 'feel' or 'know' something.

Oftentimes, this is what the Bible calls the "distinguishing' or 'discerning of spirits', or 'discernment', depending on your translation.[56] The Greek word translated 'distinguishing' or 'discerning' literally means to pass judgement, and 'spirits' is the word *pneuma* which can apply to Holy Spirit, the human spirit or evil spirits. Therefore discernment is the supernatural gift of being able to make an assessment as to the root spirit behind a behaviour or occurrence. Simply put, discernment is working out if something is from God, from a person, or from the enemy.

Because of the nature of this gift, it is best used in the context of community and team. After all, we can all feel something that isn't really there! Some have used the label of 'discernment' to spiritualise and justify criticism, division, ostracism, manipulation or condemnation. Others have reduced discernment to be something only ever used in the context of demon-hunting in deliverance ministry, or for critiquing doctrine and teaching. If this gift is, in fact, a gift for unveiling, then anything we 'discern' should be shared with those in spiritual authority to weigh and act upon as they feel is appropriate. This gift should also lead us to secret prayer and conversation with God as to what His will is, so we can pray prophetically into the situation He has allowed us to discern. If He has shown us something, there must be a purpose to it.

---

[56] 1 Corinthians 12:10

A number of years ago, I was a leader of a student ministry, which was made up of all the eighteen to thirty-somethings in the church. They were a great bunch and God was doing some really exciting things in the group. One recurrence we had seen was the returning of backslidden believers, who had grown up in the church but drifted away in their teenage years. One day, we had a new person arrive. Like many others, he had grown up in the church but fallen away, so many of the group already knew him. He was friendly, polite and engaging, but I had something in my gut that didn't feel comfortable with him. I couldn't explain, rationalise or articulate why, but I just didn't trust him. I asked God to give me an insight into why I felt that way - was there an issue with me, perhaps jealousy? Or was I discerning something?

Within a week, one of the women in the group came to me quite upset and said that this guy had tried to reignite their previous relationship from years before, in a way that made her feel uncomfortable. She wanted advice as to how to turn down his advances gently. This guy was single and was now in a group with a number of attractive single females, so I didn't think him pursuing one of the women was a bad thing - at worst, perhaps he had just been a bit clumsy. However, over the course of the next week, I began hearing different women in the group telling how he had made a move on them or been suggestive, or flirtatious. It was almost as if God was directing these accounts to me. After the fourth occasion, I knew I needed to do something, but had no idea what - after all, He obviously wanted to be in a relationship, but wasn't going about it in a wise or godly way. As a guy, I've been there myself. But because of my gut feeling, I asked God for wisdom because I wanted to know how to talk with him and pastor this guy well. I prayed the prayer I had first prayed - "give me eyes to see." God loves to answer that prayer, even if we don't quite know what it is we're asking.

Shortly after, another woman in the group came to me wanting advice. She was a strong character and a natural leader. I had noticed she had withdrawn from the group in recent weeks and wasn't as vocal or contributing as much. It turned out that this gentleman had been pursuing her since he arrived and she had responded to his advances, so they had begun seeing a lot of each other. Of course, this put my alarm bells up because of what else I'd learned about him, plus the impact this new-found relationship had on this woman. She told me he had been putting verbal pressure on her for sex, was addicted to painkillers, smoked cannabis, and got drunk almost every night. He had a double-life, and she was asking me how she should pastor him.

Suffice it to say that my advice was pretty direct, short and involved the words 'run away now.' Things got even more clear when another gentleman, a non-believer who lived next door to one of the members of the group, had come along to a social evening we arranged. He saw the gentleman I had concerns about, and later that evening let it slip to his neighbour that he sold drugs to him!

In the space of a few days, God had unveiled some character aspects about him that confirmed that I had indeed been discerning with him and after talking with some other senior leaders, we spoke to the guy with an offer to walk with him through his issues and addictions, by discipling and pastoring him. Sadly, as a challenge sometimes does, he revealed his heart by taking offence, denying what he'd heard, aggressively rejecting our offer and stopped coming to anything.

I share that story because part of discernment involves one of the most difficult forms of trust - self-trust. That is why it is key to share anything you think may be discernment with a trusted, mature leader. Don't make snap decisions on your own, because you risk either ignoring what could be God speaking, or taking an erroneous thought and letting it develop into suspicion and judgmentalism.

Prophetic Sensations

Often associated with words of knowledge, which is when something about someone is prophetically made known, prophetic sensations can be something felt in your physical body. Perhaps you become aware of a certain part of your body through a tingling or other unusual feeling. For me, I'll just feel part of my body tingle, like it had electricity running through it. This sounds bizarre yet it isn't painful - and it draws my attention to that part of my body. This opens up the conversation with God as to why I'm aware of this body part and is it Him making me aware? Is He giving me a word of knowledge for healing for that part of the body? Or is my lunch manifesting itself in an unusually comical way?

On one occasion I was ministering in a small house group setting, and during worship became acutely aware of my heartbeat. At the same time, I felt a whisper in my spirit say 'heart murmur'. It was easy to ignore the whisper, but whilst my heart wasn't pounding and I wasn't in pain, I could just 'sense' my heart in an unusual way. When I say unusual, what I mean is that I don't normally have an awareness of my heart in the same way I did at that moment. I stepped out in faith and asked if anyone in the group of about ten had a heart murmur, and a woman present responded, saying she had been diagnosed with one the day before, and that morning had taken medication for it for the first time. This opened up an opportunity to pray for her healing.

On occasion, I'll hear an accompanied word - sometimes a medical condition - or I'll see part of the body, like a heart or ear. For example, at one meeting I became aware of the top of my right foot and saw the word 'metatarsal', which I know are the bones in the foot. I shared the word and a couple of people responded as those who had some kind of damaged metatarsal. You don't have to use medical terminology - you might not see anyone confirm they have a damaged scapula, but they might be more likely to understand you when you say that God wants to heal busted shoulders!

Of course, we need to be aware of our own bodies so as not to confuse God speaking with the questionable food we've just eaten, the lack of sleep we're experiencing, or the funny aches and pains that we can get some cold or wet days. But ultimately, if you get a sensation in your body, go with it. It might be the first step towards someone receiving a healing!

Practising The Prophetic

If we want God to show us things to sense, it's a good idea to consecrate our emotions, minds and bodies to Him. Take some time to speak with Him and see if there is anything you currently think about or physically do that He wants to discuss with you - for example, certain actions or topics of contemplation. What we do with our bodies matters, as does what we think about and dwell on. Then repent. Whether there is something or not that God has put his finger on, place your hands on your heart and head and pray a prayer of dedication that your heart and mind belong to Him, and ask Him to extend your spiritual antenna to sense all that He wants you to sense. Expect to feel new things with your natural and spiritual senses!

11. Avoiding Crossed Wires

I used to work as a Pastor for an American mega-church and a number of my colleagues come from outside the United States. The team that I managed had team members where English was their second or even third language. Add in the differences between American and British English, and there is a lot of potential for confusion. Hailing from the south of England, near London - by American standards close to London, but by British standards not so much - my accent, dialect and idioms were not universal even to the other British staff members. Sometimes I would slip into slang or figures of speech particular to the area I grew up in, and the people I grew up around. It was often at this point that many of my colleagues would look at me quizzically! I started having to backtrack and explain myself to help keep the communication lines flowing, but over time as I learned to adapt my communications my colleagues began to understand me better. To ensure the message communicated is the message received and understood, an element of *interpretation* had to take place.

Interpretation is connected to culture, which is why translation and interpretation are two different things. If I take the French term *pomme de terre* and translate it literally, in English it would mean 'apple of the earth', as *pomme* is apple and *terre* is earth. Not everyone may know what an apple of the earth is, or they might even assume they know and come up with all sorts of conclusions! But if I *interpret* that phrase correctly, I know that whilst it has a different literal meaning, it is actually the French wording for potato.

Spend time with people who are not like you and it soon becomes evident that we all wear eyeglasses that influence how we see and hear things, and therefore understand them. This is why people can see an event and have utterly different opinions about it. Nationality, family, education, values, political and religious beliefs and traditions are all influences on our individual lens. We need to understand that even the prophetic revelation we receive flows through this lens.

Translation is a science, whereas interpretation is more of an art. Translation is technical and knowledge-based while interpretation works best with a familiarity that only comes with experience. I was leading a ministry team in Mexico and as I'm not a Spanish speaker, I needed a translator. I was paired with a young woman who would listen to me say a sentence or two, then repeat them in Spanish to the audience. At the beginning of our time together, the translation process was awkward because she wasn't familiar with how I preach - my rhythm, my pace, my emphasis, or how I build towards points. Also, some of the words I would use didn't necessarily have a direct translation into Spanish so there were times when she would have to stop me and ask what I meant. I'd explain it to her and she could choose the best language to capture the concept. Translation felt slow and frustrating at first, but by the end of our time, having heard and translated most of my sermons, she knew what I was building up to or what I was meaning with my phraseology. She was able to **interpret** me, as well as translate.

Correct interpretation, then, requires repeated exposure and encounter to best understand a heart. It follows that accurate prophetic interpretation is immediately rooted in our relationship with God. We may well get revelation but unless we learn how to correctly interpret them, we aren't actually going to prophesy correctly.

God often speaks through pictures, which bring with them some interesting dynamics. Symbols all have a meaning attached to them, but they aren't universal. Our nationality, age, culture and personal bias will all influence how we interpret a visual symbol. For example, in some nations, red is a colour associated with danger and alarm. Roadside warning signs are painted red to catch drivers' attention to warn them of risks ahead. In other nations, however, red is connected to prosperity and wealth. To wear red or paint a building red is to make a statement of actual, or desired social standing. Imagine the confusion, and possible misunderstanding, if we always interpreted any red symbol as being a warning or a hazard. Conversely, what if we were attracted to pursue something red because we assumed it was a desirable object?

Another interesting example is snakes. For many, snakes are bad news. I lived in the rugged and rocky landscape of northern California for five years, which is a snake utopia. Any serpent in my eyeline needed to be behind a foot-thick shield of perspex. Many of us are wary of snakes. We might justify our snake-phobia by remembering about the evil serpent in Eden who misled Adam and Eve. Or we simply ponder fangs, hissing, slithering and flesh-melting venom. However we are wired, generally, in the West, snakes are not positive symbols. If you aren't convinced, call someone a 'snake' and see how they react.

Yet in some cultures, snakes are considered good! To the ancient Greeks, snakes were considered symbols of wisdom and linked to physicians and healing. The rod of Asclepius may not be something we know by name, but we all recognise it - it is a rod entwined with a serpent, ascribed to their demigod of healing, and is used by many medical organisations and facilities because of its historic symbolism. Jesus used the example of being 'wise like serpents'[57] when encouraging his disciples. Even biblically, the symbol of a snake can have more than one interpretation.

The Bible is full of examples of God speaking to people through imagery, in things like dreams and visions, so an understanding of symbols and images is important. Since we all associate symbols with meanings, we need to be aware of how we interpret symbols. We should ask ourselves firstly, what could the symbol mean scripturally? Secondly, is God using the symbol in the same way we would? If we make a leap of assumption, we will, in fact, literally not get the message. Even if we get the correct revelation, we shouldn't think we've necessarily interpreted it correctly.

[57] Matthew 10:16

Practising The Prophetic

Ask God to indicate to you a person in your life. You might see their face, hear their name, or just sense who this person is. Once you know who it is, ask God to give you a picture for them. Ask specifically for a picture, which might be a single image or a movie. Ask God to give you clarity on the imagery He shows you - what does it mean to Him? Does that line up with what your immediate thought would have been? Repeat this exercise for four other people, taking the time to see if your natural interpretation of the images differs from what God says they mean after you've prayed. Then go and share the encouraging prophetic words with the people God spoke to you about!

12. Joining the Dots

Interpreting revelation is both relational and practical. Knowing the heart of God helps us discern the meaning, but there are certain things we can do to help us in the interpretative process. There are four factors I consider 'good practice' to consider when looking to understand a revelation I've received.

Firstly, correctly **stewarding a revelation** is key. Have you ever heard someone share a word and it feels like it is incomplete? Perhaps what was shared didn't feel appropriate at the time it was spoken - it just didn't fit with the tenor or sense of the moment. Maybe the meaning was unclear or even unknown? Sometimes people will receive a picture or word, but not get the fullness of it and share it before it is ready - for example, "I see a picture of a staircase going up but I don't know what it means." Receiving revelation is the first step of the prophetic journey; the second step is knowing what the interpretation is. There are times when God speaks to me, but I don't know what He is saying! On those occasions, I hold the revelation in my spirit, sometimes write it down, and ask God for the meaning. Without a meaning, the revelation is a lot less likely to make sense to the recipient. Dialoguing with God about the revelation will improve our accuracy and sharpness. This process of dialoguing might only take a few moments, but it might take days, weeks or even longer! The best wines take the longest to mature, and some prophetic words need the watering of prayer and reflection to fully understand the meanings. You may feel strongly that God has shown you a picture for a person of a dancing hippopotamus, and you may well be accurately hearing from God, but without an interpretation, you'll simply be a conduit for confusion and mystery instead of a voice of encouragement. How many prophetic words have been shared 'half-baked' because we've either been too zealous to prophesy, or we've been fearful of what people might think if we don't have something good to say, so we just say something? Of course, there will be occasions where a picture without meaning makes sense to the hearer but as a general rule of thumb, I would caution speaking out words without getting an interpretation for them. I've fallen into this trap many times. Once, I was praying for a young man and kept seeing a guitar. Rather than sit and wait, I blurted out "I see a guitar, does that mean anything to you?". He looked at me quizzically and politely smiled, but said it did not. Whilst no damage was done other than to my pride, which is never a bad thing, I wonder what ministry opportunity I had impacted by speaking instead of listening.

Secondly, we must ensure that we **minimise prophetic alteration**. Remember the crazy charismatic Corinthian church Paul had to keep in line? In his first letter to them, he told them that 'we all prophesy in part.'[58] This means that not everything we prophesy will actually be correct! Our prophetic words are a mixture of correctly interpreted revelation from God's Spirit to our spirit, and our own interpretation or addition of information. Prophetic maturity, then, is partly that as we grow in our gift we are able to correctly discern what comes from God and what comes from us, and filter out that which we have added to God's intended message. Understanding this will help us ponder the prophetic humbly, and protect us from seeing ourselves as the all-knowing, all-seeing prophet to the nations who

---

[58] 1 Corinthians 13:9

has yet to be discovered or recognised by those around us! Early in my Christian life, as I was learning how to prophesy, a seasoned minister took me aside one day and told me he noticed that when I prophesied, I repeated myself. I would share my revelation and my interpretation, and then say the same interpretation but a different way, with some other things added on. He gently encouraged me to reflect on whether I was getting further revelation as I spoke, which can and does happen sometimes, or if I was simply 'adding in fluff' to feel like I was saying more. At first I was offended, but sure enough, he was right. In my insecurity, rather than just stopping talking, I would repeat and inevitably, and unwillingly, add things. His wider point was that by adding fluff, I was at risk of obscuring the truth that God wanted to say behind all my unneeded verbiage.

Thirdly, **developing spiritual self-awareness** is essential in helping us minister well prophetically. If we know ourselves, we can recognise the possible influences that could colour or flavour what we share. We are persons comprised of material and immaterial parts. These parts all influence each other. Our material brain is influenced by our immaterial mind, while our immaterial mind can be influenced by our material brain chemistry. Some mental health issues exist because of imbalanced brain chemistry, for example. Our physical body can influence how we prophesy. I know that if I am hungry, I run the risk of not only interpreting incorrectly, but all my revelations start becoming pictures of burgers, steaks and fries. Perhaps it is a coincidence that God speaks to me through foodstuffs when I'm hungry, or perhaps my body is telling me something! Tiredness and fatigue are also considerations. The more tired we are, the more our prophetic process will be influenced.

As well as our body, our mind and emotions can play their part. Strong emotions will certainly be an influence. If we are prophesying whilst angry, frustrated, feeling hopeless, cynical or negative, fearful or stressed, then failure to recognise and compartmentalise those emotions will fail to represent God's heart and won't serve the recipient of the prophetic word.

If we have agendas, opinions or desires for the intended recipient, these can spill over and shape the prophetic word. I know of an account of a young man who felt that God had told him that a certain young woman was called to be his wife. He drummed up the courage to walk up to her at church one day and told her that God had spoken to him about her. She looked at him and calmly said "Thank you. God hasn't told me that though. Nor has he told my husband who is over there.." Needless to say, the young man had let his desires shape his word.

For this reason, I'm cautious when prophesying over close friends or family members. We often have opinions for those with whom we share a heart connection. I prefer to offer what I am feeling as my personal opinion, not a prophecy. That way, there is security - it's hard for someone to disagree or go against the counsel of the Lord, but pretty easy to disagree with me and ignore my advice!

Fourthly, we do well to **avoid assumption**. Another interpretative error is when we assume that we know what a revelation means, particularly when it is a symbol or picture. I once sat next to a woman who wore a wonderful purple dress. I couldn't ignore it, and for me, when something 'nags' me in the spirit, I've learned that it is the Lord drawing my attention somewhere because He wants to speak to me through it. I know that in the cultural times of the Bible, purple would be a colour worn by figures of royalty or imperial ranking because it was expensive due to the rarity and cost of producing purple dye, so I prophesied over her she was a princess of heaven, a queen, and she had rank, influence and authority in the Kingdom. All because of her purple dress. When I had finished my purple-inspired homily, she thanked me and told me that what I said was nice, but she wasn't sure about it all. She said that God often spoke to her through colours, and purple meant something different to her than what I had shared. As she spoke, I felt a conviction - I had just assumed my interpretation of the colour purple was the same as the Lord's at that moment. It's not that God doesn't use my knowledge of symbols or colours, but He certainly isn't limited or restricted by it - if I have ears to hear what it is He wants to say. Bottom line: always check in with the Lord, instead of assuming we know what He means.

In summary, it is entirely possible to have a correct revelation from God, but an incorrect interpretation of it. We've heard God correctly but not necessarily understood Him clearly. But what if we have interpreted Him correctly? What do we do now? This leads us to the third part of prophecy: the application.

Practising The Prophetic

Look over the four interpretative principles in this chapter - stewarding the revelation, minimising prophetic alteration, developing spiritual self-awareness, and avoiding assumption. Do you see any that you are susceptible to? In which ones are you strongest, and in which ones are you weakest? Make a prayerful commitment to develop the one you feel you need to grow in the most.

13. Speaking the King's English

After revelation and interpretation, the third step in the prophetic process is the application. It is a word connected to action. Whenever we apply ourselves to do something, we focus on it. If we want a new job, we send in an application. If I want to check my email on my phone, I open up the app - the application - and can see emails from many people in Africa and America who want to send me millions and millions if I only send them a few hundred first.

In the same way, we have prophetic application. What do we do, now that we have received a revelation and walked through the process of interpretation? What's next? How do we apply - action - what we are considering? Whatever we may be believing God is saying, our chosen action in light of the interpreted revelation we carry must be clothed in love. Scripture tells us that 'a word aptly spoken is like apples of gold in settings of silver.'[59] It is pleasing to the senses and brings strength. What we say is important, but just as essential is *how* we say it. It is entirely possible to receive a correct revelation, interpret it correctly, and then deliver the prophetic word in a way that actually destroys the desired effect!

Paul was very familiar with the crazy charismatic Corinthian church, who were such prophesying machines that they were speaking over each other, often interrupting one another to share the revelations

[59] Proverbs 25:11

they had. It was such bedlam that Paul tried to instruct them to bring order to their meetings because the power of each prophecy would be lost if they weren't being heard.[60] Despite some teachings or examples, prophesying is not a case of possession by Holy Spirit. He is gentle and doesn't force Himself on the person He wants to speak through. Instead, prophesying is another example of us partnering with God. He loves to work with his children. He doesn't need to, of course, but instead chooses to because He values intimacy. Intimacy is a result of love and God is Love,[61] so everything He involves Himself in is so that He can express His love, including His co-labouring with us.

It is interesting that amongst Paul's instructions, he teaches that 'the spirits of prophets are subject to prophets.'[62] Self-control is a fruit of the Spirit, so it makes little sense for Holy Spirit to then take control over someone that He is encouraging to flourish in self-control! I've encountered people who have said they 'just had to speak' and seemed to feel the urge to 'prophesy' any time, any moment, whether appropriate or not.

I once had the unfortunate experience of entering into a conversation with a gentleman who phoned me seeking advice. In my role at the time, I was involved with oversight of a number of churches so would often speak with leaders about issues they faced, which sometimes meant talking about issues they faced with other leaders! This gentleman phoned me up to share concerns he had with a leader of a church. After a long judgemental and slanderous monologue

---

[60] 1 Corinthians 14:29-33

[61] 1 John 4:16

[62] 1 Corinthians 14:32

talking at me about this church leader - the first red flag - he finally allowed me to speak. I asked him how long he had been a leader in the church, and he replied that he only visited the church once - the second red flag. Incredulous that he had phoned me up to in effect slander a leader, I challenged him about his heart attitude. I then proceeded to receive a shouting and abusive rant down the phone accusing me of all the same things he had only just been saying about the church leader he originally called about! This was the third and final red flag, and I told him that if he didn't rein in his emotions and speak to me civilly, I would end the conversation. He shouted more, and I hung up. He phoned me back straight away, and I answered, partly because I thought he might apologise. But no, he wanted to shout some more. I hung up again, turned my phone to silent, and went for a walk to calm down. When I came back to my phone fifteen minutes later, I saw that I had **seven** voicemails, each of at least two minutes long. All from him. I listened to the first five seconds of the first message, which began with the phrase "this is no longer a man speaking, this is the voice of the Living God." Needless to say, I stopped listening, deleted all the messages and blocked his number.

Any impact this gentleman may have hoped his words would have on me was totally diminished by what could only be described as the accompanying word-vomit, hysteria and extreme nasal breathing. If the spirit of prophets is subject to prophets, then this principle must also be true for those of us who do not move in a prophet's anointing, authority or level of gifting. It means we can control, manage or even stop prophetic utterance. God has given us an incredible privilege and responsibility to influence and control the flow and delivery of prophecy in and through us. Now, some would have us believe that to do this would be to quench the Holy Spirit but if that was so, why would Paul - who also wrote about what it meant to quench the Spirit - instruct the Corinthians to wait their turn to prophesy? I understand that there are 'burdens of the Lord' (for example, Jeremiah felt a 'burning in his bones' with the word of the Lord he carried[63]) but even then, Jeremiah still had the ultimate choice regarding the manner of prophetic application. I propose that people who cannot regulate when or how they prophesy - irrespective of the accuracy of their revelation or interpretation - are acting less out of a spirit-led source and more out of one that is human - spiritually immature or fleshly. Worst-case-scenario, if they truly feel they have no control, it might even be something demonic.

To be effective messengers in the prophetic, I've developed an ABCDE of prophetic delivery good practice which is beneficial in ensuring we speak wisely and speak well. When prophesying, we do well when we are mindful of our **authenticity**, **brevity**, **clarity**, **delivery** and **externals**.

Authenticity refers to us being genuine and real in how we share. Being authentic in our prophesying means being ourselves. God speaks through us and doesn't want robots or empty vessels, but wants to work with and through us. When we read the prophetic books of the Bible, we can see aspects of their personality in their writings. For example, we can see through some of his writings that Isaiah has a somewhat sarcastic humour about him. Did God overrule that, or did He speak to Isaiah because of how Isaiah would interpret and communicate the revelations God showed him? Prophecy is a partnership between God and man so being ourselves is important, otherwise, our words will feel false or fake.

---

[63] Jeremiah 20:9

It is also wise to understand and communicate that we are so authentic, we acknowledge that we can sometimes be authentically wrong! It's good practice to use language like, 'I feel God is saying' or, 'I think God is saying' rather than the more definitive 'God says'. This approach is humble, gives room for correction and also acknowledges that we prophesy in part. Otherwise, there is no room for disagreement, and this can lead to prophecy being used to control others - others whom Holy Spirit is teaching to grow in self-control, not by-others-be-controlled!

I knew a gentleman who lived in a house with some other single men, and after the inescapable honeymoon period of manly wrestling, marathon movie nights, constant video games and junk food consumption expired, personality clashes and conflicts began to take place. One day, the aforementioned gentleman, who didn't really ever properly work through disagreements or conflicts with others, announced that the Lord had spoken and he was moving out. Perhaps Jesus did speak to him, or perhaps Jesus really wanted him to grow in character and relational skills by working through issues with others. Ultimately it didn't seem to matter; he believed he had received a word from God, and it's pretty hard to reason with someone who is adamant they have heard 100% clearly from the All-Knowing, All-Seeing One, who just so happens to have taken their side in the discussion.

By **brevity**, I mean getting to the point. Don't take longer than you need to. Don't say the key points twice! One of my prophetic mentors told me that a useful rule of thumb is to listen to prophetic words because when they start to repeat themselves it may be that the first part is God, the second part is man. It's a guide, not a rule, but worth considering. I also don't want to write a paragraph about brevity and be long myself.

Clarity ensures that we make the prophetic point clear. What exactly is God saying? There are times when people will share the entire backstory of how God spoke to them, including every minute detail. Such detail can obscure the heart of what God wants to say through the prophetic word, so it is a good discipline to self-edit what we say. Clarity is often linked to brevity, as I explained above. Unnecessary details will simply bring in a fog of confusion, requiring the hearer to filter through our words. Forcing people to have to interpret our prophecies doesn't seem conducive to powerful and effective ministry! Simply put, the more we say, the more there is that could potentially distract or confuse people from the essence of the message.

Our **delivery** matters. Words are powerful, but how we say them can contradict the very thing we are trying to communicate. Consider tone, volume and language in your delivery. Does God only speak through English from the Kings James Version? I watched a woman I knew prophesy a number of times. For some reason, whenever she spoke what she felt God was saying, she seemed to undergo a spiritual personality transplant at the same time which affected her voice: she would speak in a slow and, quite frankly, robotic tone. It was rather amusing, even more so when she was speaking about the joy of heaven whilst everyone else was feeling anything but. Delivery matters!

Our **externals** are in essence, our body language. Ideally, it should reinforce what our mouth says. However, we all know times when someone is saying one thing while their body is saying something else entirely. "I'm not angry at you," spoken with closed fists and furrowed brow will send mixed signals to anyone. So it is with the prophetic. Do our mannerisms, manifestations or body language echo or erase our words? Are we saying one thing with our words, and another with our eyes, our posture, or our arms? Consider the timing of the sharing of the word as well; does it fit with the spiritual moment you are in? Some words need to be stewarded, pondered, meditated on and considered. This is certainly true for corporate words shared during public meetings of any size. Revelation does not necessarily indicate a green light for immediate sharing. Maybe the Lord is generating something in you that won't be ready for 'birthing' for a number of minutes, or days, or weeks, or even months or years.

In summary, our prophetic application can actually make or break what we are trying to say. If we are wise, our message can be received loud and clear. If we aren't, then the heart of God is lost amongst the static of our failed transmission. This part of the process shows us clearly the responsibility and privilege of partnering with God, and whilst it may feel an overwhelming burden, it is actually amazing that God wants not only to work with us but to train us to be effective in our ministry with Him. We can see that receiving correct revelation is one thing, but it still needs to be interpreted correctly, then applied and delivered well. Each of these steps shapes our prophetic communications in positive or negative ways. It is worth reminding ourselves of this as we seek to steward the prophetic messages the Lord gives us for others so that we accurately represent not only His words but also His heart.

Practising The Prophetic

Look over the ABCDE principles in this chapter - authenticity, brevity, clarity, delivery and externals. In which ones are you strongest, and in which ones are you weakest? Make a prayerful commitment to develop the one you feel you need to grow in the most.

14. Prophetic Gateways

Being British, I grew up in a land full of castles. I know it seems to non-Europeans that many of us live in castles, or there is one on every street, but I assure you that this isn't the case. Yet, they aren't uncommon across the UK. Some castles are in great conditions and are even liveable, and some are simply broken down walls that are centuries old. An interesting thing about castles is that there is a clear entrance/exit. Some castles may have moats, which are big trenches that require a bridge to cross over. Other castles have drawbridges, which are huge doors that double as bridges across the moat if there is one. Bigger castles have portcullises, which are huge metal gates that add strength and protection behind the drawbridge. All of these openings would have been heavily guarded. In effect, the castle entrance controlled who could come in, who could go out, and when.

In the same way, it is good for us to be aware of the 'gates' that we should ensure our prophetic utterances 'pass through' before we speak them out. We have a role and responsibility as a gatekeeper to ensure our words pass some internal tests. If our words don't pass the standard of the gate, we may need to slam shut the portcullis or drawbridge until our words can meet the required standard! Let me propose five of these tests, or gates if you will.

Gate 1: Biblically Sound

Whilst it seems obvious, it is always worth stating that the authority of prophetic words never trumps the authority of the written word, the Bible. In fact, all authority of prophecy comes from the authority of scripture. It's actually great practice to prophesy scripture - by that, I mean having words shaped by the teachings and heart of the Bible. It doesn't just mean prophesying full verses - although that isn't a bad thing in itself - but it means giving prophetic words littered with illustrations from scripture, or shedding insights on verses, bringing fresh light and life to what God has written for generations. These revelations should never contradict the teachings of the scriptures but should honour the spirit of the Bible. Whilst not all prophecy will be found in the pages of the Bible, all prophecy will honour the Bible in teaching and spirit. The same Author of the Bible is the same Inspirer of prophecy. If we have a disparity in our revelations, then perhaps we haven't received or interpreted the revelation correctly. It is for this reason that both the prophet and the teacher need each other. The best preaching and teaching is always prophetic in nature, imitating Jesus on the road to Emmaus. He interpreted the words of scripture in a fresh, powerful way that revealed the heart and mind of God in such a manner that it caused the hearers' hearts to burn within them. His words were anointed by the power and presence of Holy Spirit and anchored in the scriptures.

It is sobering to read the words James wrote to his readers that those who teach will be judged more strictly[64], because it is entirely possible to employ the skill-sets of analysis, research, background reading, communication theory and structure, and public speaking, to deliver a sermon of an informed and educational level, all without any anointing. Factually correct, but like dry bread. As preachers and teachers, we need not only to be shaped by the prophetic externally through others but also internally by hearing God ourselves Spirit to spirit, letting His words shape our interpretation of the Word. When our hearers listen to us, do their hearts burn within them?

[64] James 3:1

Conversely, as prophetic ministers, it is also entirely possible to speak words that seem mystical, deep, insightful or spiritual, but actually have no grounding or grasp of the principles, precepts and heart of scripture. They are 'spiritual fluff', much like a dandelion seed that is caught up by the wind, attracting a momentary smile of wonder then almost immediately fading from memory and relevance as it is blown away in an unknown direction by some passing gust of air. In my experience, the best prophetic ministers - accurate and effective in their ministry, and both longstanding and long lasting - eat, live, breathe, consume, feed on, meditate on, and burn for, the scriptures. Let us seek to live with this standard, that our understanding of scripture forever expands so it provides a covering, ceiling and filter for any and all prophetic revelations we may feel we have.

Gate 2: Represents the Heart of the Father

If prophecy seeks to comfort, strengthen and encourage and is the testimony of Jesus - Him saying what He sees - then it follows that our words should seem, sound and feel like words that Jesus Himself would say. The Father is exactly that: a father, and a good Father. Paul tells the Romans that the Kingdom of God - the realm influenced by the rule and reign of God - is righteousness, peace and joy in the Holy Spirit.[65] God is a joyful God, a God of peace, and a God of righteousness, which means that prophecy should be something that brings joy, brings peace and brings righteousness. The first two of these three are self-evident, but what does it mean for prophetic words to bring righteousness?

---

[65] Romans 14:17

When we examine the scriptural Hebrew and Greek words connected to the concept of righteousness, we see that they contain the ideas of agreement or alignment with God's normal. Simply put, righteousness is agreement with or alignment to the standards God has established. God doesn't look at things in the same way as humans do. We tend to view things as right or wrong, or good or bad, for example. God sees things as righteous or unrighteous, stating whether or not they are in agreement with His heart. It follows then that scripture, and therefore prophecy should reveal His heart. When God declares someone or something righteous or unrighteous, He is acting as Judge and is making a judgement. Because He is a righteous judge, His judgements are always righteous. However, God doesn't just make judgements; He acts on His judgements to bring about justice. Justice, then, which is closely connected to righteousness, can be defined as any act by man or God that brings righteousness to an unrighteous situation. The Cross of Christ was the supreme act of justice in history because unrighteous sinners were given the opportunity to become righteous saints. Prophecy should reveal righteousness by showing people how God sees them, or their circumstances. In effect, prophecy reveals the righteous heart of God and invites us to repent and align our beliefs into agreement with his judgements.

To illustrate this practically, let us consider a believer who struggles with believing that God loves them unconditionally. When we minister to them by speaking the love of God to them, there is an invitation available for them to repent from unrighteous beliefs, renew their mind and embrace righteous thinking. The result is that the individual is strengthened, built up, encouraged and comforted - the purpose of prophecy - and the fruit is joy, peace and righteousness. As believers, we stand before God legally righteous in

Christ. We have been justified, meaning that the justice of God has been applied to us to make us righteous. Even so, we don't always believe or behave righteously. Prophecy is a means of grace to us that enables and empowers us to live in alignment with the heart of Heaven. When we let the prophetic influence our thinking, we actually align with God's heart and His purposes. Knowing how God sees us should change how we see ourselves, and therefore change how we live.

Gate 3: Shared In A Loving Way

Certain scripture verses seem to be embedded in the psyche of many believers, who use them as weapons to reinforce their own personal sense of mission. Often this is essential for purpose, faith and focus. On occasion though, it can be a negative experience for everyone else, who ends up being at the receiving end of a proof-text used out of context. One such example is 'speaking the truth in love.'[66] It seems to me that most of the time when someone quotes that verse at me, it is because they are about to bring some correction or rebuke to me, and not only that but the experience is going to be anything other than loving! Funnily enough, the context of that half-verse (ignoring the point that quoting a half-verse often misses out on key information that shapes our interpretation of it!) is connected to maturity, for the church to be like Christ. Simply put, truth and love are not a choice of either/or but a connection of both/and. Warren Wiersbe, a phenomenal Bible teacher, scholar and author, says, "love without truth is hypocrisy, but truth without love is brutality." We would do really well to ensure our prophetic words are not only delivered in a loving way, but coloured and influenced by the love of the Father, and our love for the recipient. I would challenge that if

[66] Ephesians 4:15

we don't love the recipient, it is better not to prophesy over them until we see them with the same love that the Father does.

Gate 4: Without Agenda or Motive

I believe in prophetic pastoring, which I understand to be prophetic insights or words of knowledge that unlock a pastoral or counselling situation. I don't like the 'prophetic pastoring' that can take place when someone wants to bring advice or counsel - often uninvited - and wraps it up in prophetic language. For example, someone once brought a prophetic word to me which didn't have any interpretation or make any sense. I asked them to reconsider it and come back to me with more, because I really wanted to hear the heart of God for me, and I wanted this person, who had a prophetic gifting, to grow. She came back to me the next week and said she didn't have anything more with that word, but actually had a new word for me. The new word was a picture of a field that was rammed full of seeds ripe for harvest, full to the edges, and the interpretation was a verse from Leviticus about not gleaning all the crops from the harvest, but leaving room for others to glean.[67] Her understanding of this was for me to leave room for people to glean as well, and that I shouldn't be black or white in my pastoral leadership. Irrespective of whether she was right or wrong, it felt like she was using prophecy as a shield to hide behind so she could share her opinion without actually being open to the possibility of dialogue or a differing opinion. I'm sure you can see the dangers of our agendas or desires being verbalised behind a 'thus says the Lord' form of communication.

---

[67] Leviticus 23:22

Paul told the Roman church that one sign of our divine adoption is that we would be led by the Spirit of God.[68] Any healthy father would speak to his children directly first before involving others. Perhaps God doesn't want me to do this, or doesn't want me to do that, but I'm not sure that He would speak to someone who shares the same opinion, and has a stake or interest in my actions, and use that person's bias or agenda to bring direction to me through a prophetic word. As a leader, without a doubt, there are times when I have needed to bring something of concern to someone I'm leading, but I don't shroud it in prophecy. Instead, I am clear that this is my interpretation and opinion, even if I feel that it is an insight from God; I prophesy in part, after all. Bottom line: if you are emotionally invested in someone, either their person or their actions, don't prophesy your opinion. Share your opinion for what it is - the opinion of a person. This is actually a biblical principle! In 1 Corinthians 7, Paul is giving the sexually liberal Corinthian church some love life advice, both to pre-marrieds and marrieds. In verse 25, he writes about a subject, in effect saying, 'in this, I have no command from the Lord, but I definitely have an opinion.' The Apostle Paul! He knew some things he wrote came from a place of revelation, but it seems some things were considered opinions; he didn't claim Divine opinion if it was his opinion. We would do well to discern the difference and speak in the same way.

Gate 5: Lead People Into Encounter

If prophecy reveals the heart of God, which is a heart of love, then it follows that upon receiving a healthy prophetic word, it should be easy for the recipient to step into praise, thanksgiving and worship. What is said should unveil something about God that makes them

---

[68] Romans 8:14

feel good! From here, worship is the right heart response and Psalms tells us, we enter God's presence through thanksgiving and celebration.[69] He draws near to gratitude, and we encounter Him when we celebrate who He is and what He has done. Angry, rebuking, harsh or stern prophetic words aren't going to encourage people to approach a throne of grace. Instead, they will give them reasons to flee from a throne of judgement. If we leave our prophetic recipients more in love with Jesus, then we have done well.

These five gates are by no means exhaustive, and there could be more you feel are beneficial. At the very least though, they are essential guidelines to ensure we communicate the heart of God well. Communication or transmission is only half of the process though; what about receiving prophecy? How do we consider prophetic words spoken to us by others? We'll look at that next.

Practising The Prophetic

Look over the five prophetic gateways in this chapter for giving prophetic words - being biblically sound, representing the heart of the Father, sharing in a loving way, sharing without agenda or motive, and leading people into an encounter. In which ones are you strongest, and in which ones are you weakest? Make a prayerful commitment to develop the one you feel you need to grow in the most.

---

[69] Psalm 100

15. Trying & Testing

Whenever anyone with a recognised prophetic ministry is around and begins to minister, a myriad of reactions can be observed in people. Some of us shrink down in our seats, trying to avoid eye contact with the man or woman with the microphone, just in case they can see all our sin and then publicly chastise us in front of all our friends, shaming us into stopping kicking the dog, burning the dinner, or failing to put our rubbish in the recycling bin. Others sit up straight, growing an extra foot in height, trying to catch the minister's eyes but really staring them out in a quite disconcerting and stalker-ish manner. Interestingly, these people always seem to be extroverts. Then we have one more category, which is my personal favourite. These beloved brothers and sisters will wear prophetically bright and visible colours like luminous yellow, deep purple or retina-shredding orange, or clothing with everyday images like eagles, lions, doves, rainbows and other standard charismatic Christian symbols. Make-up will be bold, blue and bright - for the women as well - and you will normally see either a tambourine or a shofar in close proximity. These are not just extroverts, oh no. They are EXTROVERTS, in the most extreme, shouty, blatant kind of way. They crave, desire and *demand* a prophetic word, and before the entirety of Christendom, will do whatever it takes to get one, including flirting with behaviour that in the real world would result in a restraining order.

Whether we are picked out publicly by the prophetic person, or a word comes through more personal, private and low-profile means, how do we establish whether God is speaking to us or not? Do we accept everything said to us as the Voice of God? What do we do with those random or inaccurate communications? Fortunately, the Apostle Paul gave instructions in this area to the Thessalonian church, and those instructions can bring guidance and security to us. He writes to tell them to 'not quench the Spirit; do not despise prophecies. But test everything; hold fast what is good.'[70] There are four principles in these few verses that we can unpack to guide us to receive prophecy well.

Principle 1: Don't Quench The Spirit

Firstly, we should not quench the Spirit. The Greek word translated 'quench' here means to extinguish or snuff out. Think of a burning candle being forcefully and suddenly blown out so it no longer is able to fulfil its purpose. This is the same concept as quenching, when we extinguish or prevent the prophetic word fulfiling its purpose. Prophecy is a partnership, which means our response to it is equally a partnership; we have a say in whether prophetic words happen or not, which is very sobering! The above scripture can be another one of those oft-quoted verses used by Christians, frequently used to bring 'correction' to someone else who is doing something we don't like, or that we feel is stopping God from doing what God - or we - want. Oddly enough, church leaders can get this verse fired at them because they don't agree with a member of their church. A half-verse quoted can be inaccurate though, and in this instance, Paul qualifies *how* the Spirit is quenched. Sometimes what we *think* quenches the Spirit is purely our personal opinion or preference, because scripture itself actually tells us what quenches the Spirit!

---

[70] 1 Thessalonians 5:19-21

Principle 2: Don't Despise Prophecy

Paul links quenching the Spirit to despising prophecy. This tells us that that the primary way the Spirit is quenched is not through whether or not we have five-hour long worship sessions, or whether or not we like the pastor's preaching, but the test is in how we view and respond to prophecy. If we devalue, disrespect, dismiss or deny the existence or effectiveness of prophecy, we despise it and therefore miss out on its intended impact. We may straight away jump to consider those believers who would call themselves 'cessationist' because they believe prophecy, along with the other spiritual gifts, have ceased. However, even believers who believe in the continued existence of prophetic ministry today can quench the Spirit. How? I propose we despise prophecy when we do not listen or respond in faith to the prophetic words spoken over us as individuals or as churches. Perhaps we don't like who said it, or what was said, or we dismissed it as too little or simple. More likely, we simply forget!

I've been in church meetings where a prophetic word is shared corporately during the flow of worship, and through which God is inviting the people to encounter a certain aspect of His character - say, for example, His mercy - but the leader only verbally acknowledges or even ignores what is said. The meeting continues with the next song on the set-list, even though the song, good as it is, brings a different focus. This too is despising prophecy and quenching the Spirit. Quenching occurs when Holy Spirit is prevented from doing what He wants to do despite giving instruction through the prophetic word.

This may seem harsh to say. I don't believe any of us really set out to quench the Spirit. Yet, if we are to live Spirit-led lives, then our churches also need to be Spirit-led. By definition, this has to mean that any plans we have - and plans are a good thing - are subject to His voice. Not just in a token way, through lip service, but as a very real value. It may prove uncomfortable at times - we could sail into uncharted water, or things could get a bit messy and disorganised. Perhaps we need to change our prepared message, shorten it, or even at times scrap it! It's humbling for us as leaders to sacrifice what we have prepared but if God has spoken, it is always for a purpose[71] and so there is a response for us to make. We shouldn't manage meetings, but we should steward them. One involves inviting God to bless our gatherings, whilst with the other recognises we gather to be blessed by Him. Sometimes, when God speaks to us corporately, to use an Old Testament image, we need to stop and linger at the foot of the mountain'. It means that as leaders, we need to deploy faith and be okay with not knowing what is coming next. When we look with a kingdom perspective, that doesn't sound like a bad thing at all.

Principle 3: Test Everything

The verses in 1 Thessalonians 5 give clear biblical instruction to test prophecy. This alone should tell us that not only should prophecy be tested, but it should be tested against something. That something is scripture. Prophecy is not equal in weight or authority to the Bible. So to test prophecy well, we need to know scripture well. Any prophet who claims to have a special revelation that supersedes the Bible straight away has stepped out of an appropriate place of covering. That should sort out a few self-proclaimed prophets already! Additionally, anyone sharing a prophetic word should expect it to be weighed and judged by the recipient. I have had an occasion when someone shared something publicly that was

[71] Isaiah 55:10-11

unscriptural. She became very angry when it was communicated to her that her word would be tested and weighed. Her response was an indignant, "my prophecies *do not* need to be weighed!" Unfortunately for her, but fortunately for me, I was familiar with this aforementioned scripture and I realised that her accusations against me of unbelief, control and spiritual blindness were actually evidence of her emotional state: angry, insecure, wounded pride, all manifesting behind a veneer of false spirituality.

We really are meant to test *everything*. Every aspect of prophecy is worthy of scrutiny and consideration. This includes the revelation itself, the interpretation and the actual delivery and application. This reinforces the idea that some aspects of a word can be fine, while other aspects lack in quality. It is okay to recognise this because it provides an opportunity for growth, which is exciting both for the prophetic minister and those who would receive the benefit of their ministry. The next chapter will look in more detail at how we can test prophetic words.

Principle 4: Hold Fast Onto What Is Good

Interestingly, Paul recognises that prophetic words can be not just good, or bad, but partly good! His encouragement to hold onto the good, accurate, upbuilding and fitting elements of the prophetic word also conveys the idea to ditch, ignore, flush and forget the negative, bad or unhelpful elements of words. This means that as recipients, we don't stumble over the poor delivery of a word if it contains words that are a blessing. Whilst we should care about delivery when we are prophesying, we can be gracious to others as they step out in faith to prophesy. Discerning and being able to hold the good and overlook the bad are essential elements in honouring the prophetic. After all, we all prophesy in part, so we are all growing in this area!

In summary, there seem to be two errors we can make regarding receiving prophecy. The first error is to reject everything, which means we are quenching the Spirit and stopping Him from working in and through us to bring about what God wants. The second error is to accept everything ever said to us, no matter how bizarre, heretical, or banal. The danger here is that some 'prophecies', which aren't prophecies at all, have too much grip and influence over us. The correct attitude in weighing prophecy is to sift every word, neither rejecting all nor unquestionably accepting all. There is no guilt in rejecting or part rejecting something said to us - the Apostle Paul anticipates some words to be, simply put, not very good!

Practising The Prophetic

Consider your process for receiving prophetic words. Do you have one? If not, why not? If you do, how does it fit with the principles in this chapter? Consider applying some prophetic words you have received over your life to the principles here. Do they change how you see or interpret some of the words?

16. Setting the Scales

The verses we are discussing indicate that the responsibility and onus of weighing prophecy is always on the recipient(s). It is inappropriate for me to weigh a prophetic word I'm sharing for someone else, because I'm too attached to it; I must feel it is from God, otherwise I wouldn't be sharing it! Prophecy originates from the heart of God, meaning He will speak to His children in such a way that they can discern when He is speaking. This is encouraging, especially when seemingly random words are actually God speaking. Remember, there is always a first time for God to begin speaking about a subject!

I was once in a church meeting as a guest of a leader in the church and was sitting on the front row while the preacher - who the church accepted as a prophet to them - was speaking. He stopped his sermon and prophesied over me, speaking about an area of life that he felt God wanted to lead me into. It was an area that I had no interest in or inclination towards, wasn't functioning or operating in at the time, and I didn't care about or carry any sense of passion for. Naturally, I wasn't sure it was an accurate word. Later, I was debriefing with my friend - because community can help us test words - and said to him that the word was so out of left field that I wasn't sure it was God. My friend, the wise man that he is, suggested that it could be God for the very reason that it *was* so left-field, and proposed that God knew that I would be uncertain. He believed God would speak to me again about the subject at hand very soon so that I knew it was Him speaking to me. Funnily enough, a few days later I was at a prophetic conference and again someone prophesied over me about this same area which, as you can imagine, got my attention. Over the following week, every meeting I was in would result in a prophetic word about this area. God was getting my attention! Fast forward ten years, and whilst I'm not operating in this area yet, there have been definite seasons of acquiring skills that have led me to see how this area could unfold and open up for me. It still isn't the right season for it yet, but I'm no longer against the idea, and I would recognise opportunities or seasons connected with it that could come along. It has also become one of the most often prophesied areas of my life. It is almost as if God is saying to me, "don't forget about this, because I haven't!"

We all prophesy in part, so testing a word we've received means we scrutinise it with our minds, in prayer, with our family and friends, and with our leaders, to discern what parts of it came from the Spirit of God, and what parts don't. There are seven scales we can employ when weighing prophecy, to help us determine if it is from God, partly from God, or not from God at all.

Firstly, we should always **compare prophecy with scripture**. Any word that contradicts or violates the heart of scripture isn't a word from the Lord! Sometimes prophetic words may challenge our personal *interpretation* of scripture, but that isn't the same thing as violating the spirit of scripture. Straight-up heresy isn't from God; the unchanging God who doesn't contradict Himself or what He has revealed previously. But he might make us rethink how we've understood things!

Another principle is the **witness of our spirit**. Simply put, how did you feel when you received the word? We can't go on feelings alone, but neither should we ignore them. A lack of peace when receiving a word is certainly a red flag, unless we've already decided we don't like a prophetic word from that particular person, or about that particular subject!

It's absolutely fine to **pray about prophetic words** we receive and ask God for confirmation. Anything that invites us deeper into intimacy and connection with Him, thereby giving us an opportunity to share our heart with Him, will always be beneficial. He's a good Father, so will confirm his heart to us again and again. That might be through another prophetic word; equally, it might mean hearing the same thing through leaders or those who know us. God speaks in many ways, not just prophecy!

One trap we can fall into is weighing words according to the person sharing them. I understand this; when the world-class Christian rolls into town, with entourage in tow, pulling behind them multi-billion selling books, we want them to tell us what God says because they must have a clear line to heaven, as indicated by their success. Yet, oddly enough, God speaks through anyone He wants. On one occasion He even spoke through a donkey,[72] so that alone should humble us when we consider He is perfectly happy to speak through us. There is a difference between judging the message and judging the messenger; I wonder if many good prophetic words were ignored because of attitudes of the heart. My own experience in this area was from a time of my life when I was part of a vibrant spiritual community that, if I'm honest, had quite a few members who could be described using many words, 'vibrant' being the most pastorally kind! One such gentleman was a brusque, direct, almost comical figure - a mixture of passion, eccentricity and oddness. I'd often see him prophesy over someone, doing the prophetic shouting that combines volume with spittle, then shuffle along looking for his next

---

[72] Numbers 22:28-30

recipient - or victim, I wasn't quite sure. I rolled my eyes and portrayed gracious tolerance, but in my heart completely judged him, his motives, his gifting and his fruit. One worship time, I'm happily standing, worshipping away, when I feel a hand on my shoulder, and sense the presence of another person standing uncomfortably close, well within my personal body space. The hand was far too big to be my wife's so I peeked a glance quickly at the mysterious stranger, hoping it would be an angelic messenger bringing a directive from Heaven. It wasn't. It was him. Grinning like a Cheshire cat. Because he had a word for me.

I smiled (only on the outside, admittedly), and listened to what he said. His word can only be described as one of the most accurate, insightful and encouraging things I had heard in a long time. He knew my heart because God was speaking through him. As I listened to this love letter from Heaven, I also repented. I had totally judged this gentleman because of my religious definitions, and in doing so, would have lost out on a blessing from Heaven were it not for the intervening grace of a God who loves me enough to sometimes let me experience things that challenge how I think. So let's not judge a word because of the person speaking it. The youngest believer can share something that pierces the heart of the most mature saint. God speaks through whomever He will; remember Balaam's donkey.

Reviewing prophetic words is incredibly beneficial. Whether we keep a journal or audio files, having our prophetic history accessible helps us confirm words as we are able to compare them to the prophetic themes we've received over the years. Looking for the echoes of heaven that have been spoken to us gives us a powerful tool to weigh new words against. If we have such a record, it can strengthen us incredibly. I know a leader who keeps key words on index cards in his wallet, and whenever he has a few spare moments

- in a line at the shop, or during flight layovers, for example - he will pull out the cards and turn them into prayers. That way, he lets the prophetic shape his life in such a way that he is able to recognise quickly when God is speaking to him, whether as a confirmation or a further unpacking of the themes this leader knows are the prophetic contours of his life.

Consider the timing and seasons you are in. Some words will feel 'right' because of the moment of life you are in. Others will feel less like a 'now' word and more like a 'not yet' word. Discerning the difference helps us know how to steward and therefore respond well to each type of word.

Sometimes, we need to **look outside of ourselves**. There is a reason why God's plan is for all of us to be part of community. So don't be afraid to get a second opinion on prophetic words! Find someone trusted, wise and mature, who is for you, knows you, and isn't afraid to say the things to you that you might not want to hear. People like that are invaluable advisors.

Finally, don't be afraid to **reject out of hand prophetic words that don't fit!** Whether that is a whole word or part of a word, we can be secure and rest in the knowledge that God loves to speak and will bring something back to us that He wants us to hear. Chances are that He will say it in such a way that all doubt is removed!

Practising The Prophetic

Look over the seven scales in this chapter that help us weigh prophecy given to us - scripture, our spirit, prayer, reviewing, timing, community and filtering. In which ones are you strongest, and in which ones are you weakest? Make a prayerful commitment to develop the one you feel you need to grow in the most.

17. Response Ability

So you've received a prophetic word, weighed it, and come to the conclusion that this is indeed a word from the Lord - now what?

We do well when we remember that prophecies originate from God - at least, authentic ones do! God is committed to His word, and whenever He speaks, His words always fulfil their purpose.[73] He works to bring his prophetic declarations into existence. This should be a source of peace and comfort for us! It is equally true that because prophecy gives us an indication of the heart of God, it should stir faith in us to respond. It is a principle throughout scripture that if we hear what God says and bring ourselves into agreement with it, faith is born.[74] Genuine faith shows itself in action; which means that if no action results from hearing God speak, there is no faith present.[75] So how do we achieve the right balance of trusting God to bring about what He has promised whilst avoiding passivity? How do we respond in faith with action, without running ahead of God's timing or trying to take into our own hands the things that only He can do?!

---

[73] Isaiah 55:11

[74] Romans 10:17, for example. The immediate context for this verse is the response of faith to the gospel by those who hear it. The fact that Paul says 'faith comes from hearing..' as the first part suggests a principle we can see throughout the Bible when God speaks and it changes someone, who in turn goes on to change their world.

[75] James 2:17

At times, it is right to move forward and make things happen, so to speak - the faith response God is looking for is that we would move. On other occasions, perhaps we need to stop and rest, look to God to play His part, and wait on Him to act.[76] Western society has a hard time waiting and resting. We live in a dynamic, can-do attitude, go-getter society that champions those who chase their dreams, work hard, and make things happen. Perhaps some of our prophetic frustrations are because we have chased something in the wrong season. We have run ahead of the Lord in pursuing what isn't for today but is for tomorrow. Abraham made the same error in Genesis 16. He took the prophetic promises of God and let his frustration determine his course of action. You know the story; Hagar became his concubine and Ishmael was born - still Abraham's son no less, but not the child of promise.

The action of faith can sometimes simply be trusting. Trust leads to rest, and rest is an action. It is an intentional decision to peacefully cease moving until God leads. This is the attitude of Jesus when He said that He only did what He saw the Father doing.[77] He watched, waited and listened. Perhaps some of his disciples, including action-man Peter, thought this to be strange when they saw the need around them and began 'encouraging' and pressuring Jesus to do something. "Look at all the people!" "Look at their needs for healing and teaching!" "They've travelled all this way to hear you - don't you think you should do something for them?" Sound familiar? The pressure we put on ourselves, or even others put on us, may be well-intentioned but actually can force us to step out of sync with the Spirit. Doing something because others have said so can be down to

[76] Psalm 46:10

[77] John 5:19

our fear of man. We're concerned about what people, or a person, may think. Fear is never a good reason for doing something in the kingdom. Jesus was confident in His relationship with His Father enough to resist the pressure and expectations of his disciples and the crowd. Passivity and rest can look the same to outsiders, but the former comes from a root of fear and the latter, confidence. Interestingly, the English word 'confidence' comes from a root of two Latin words, 'con' and 'fidis'. Together, they mean 'from faith.' Godly confidence comes from a place of faith. It takes faith to rest, wait, watch and listen before acting.

Conversely, doing nothing is just as damaging to seeing the prophetic fulfiled in our lives. A laissez-faire attitude will say, 'God has spoken so it will come about' but is that necessarily true? God loves to partner with us, and the fulfilment of prophecy is one such area. Simply put, if the prophetic word over your life is to be an author of books, then your faith should demonstrate itself in writing. If you don't write, you aren't likely to get a book deal or have any work published! It might seem spiritual to 'wait on God' but even a single step forward in faith brings the prophetic fulfilment closer. A friend of mine used to say that it is easier to steer a moving ship, and he was right. God will direct our momentum once there is motion, but guess who has the privilege and responsibility of taking the first step?!

I know I've not answered the question of when we rest versus when we act. Truthfully, I can't. As is often the case, it comes down to our personal walk with God. Intimacy is key. Dialoguing with God to determine our response brings Him into our process - or rather, us into His process! A good question to ask God is this: what does obedience of faith look like in my current season? It often looks like stewardship. So what do you need to steward in faith, in connection with your prophetic words? Stewardship means faithfulness, and it is a kingdom principle that faithfulness always leads to fruitfulness. Who knows? Perhaps the faithful stewarding of your one action, or your resting, will lead to the fruit of the prophetic word blooming into existence at the right time.

I wonder how many people are acting or living in the good of something that was prophesied, but in reality was built by their own hands, using their own energy and resources. It may seem like a prophetic fulfilment but in reality is an Ishmael. In God's kindness, Ishmael was blessed, and many of the promises to Abraham concerning Isaac were also applied to Ishmael. God's heart is to see His prophetic promises come into existence through Man's faith being partnered with His power, released in His timing. Isaac was born as Abraham acted and God blessed his faith, yet Ishmael came as the result of Abraham's impatience and unbelief, which were rooted in fear. When it comes to our prophetic promises, let's not make the same mistake as Abraham and run ahead of God. We want Isaacs, not Ishmaels.

Practising The Prophetic

Consider the prophetic words over your life. What words are you acting on, and what words are you not? Are you acting on the right words? Are you sitting on the right words? Prayerfully consider if you need to change tack on your words, and what action or rest looks like.

PART III
PROPHETIC
CHARACTER

In the church I was saved into, our Sunday morning meetings had a microphone set up for public contributions, whether prayer, readings or prophetic words. During the meeting, if you felt you had something to contribute you would approach this most holy place to talk with the leaders of the church, who were on the front row of the congregation, and relate what you were feeling. They would weigh it, taking into consideration the other contributions that had either already been shared or were lined up to share, and if it fitted in with what God was saying, you would be given the nod to proceed.

I was young and so half the time, I didn't really know quite what I was doing. I knew God spoke to me, but there was often a lot of 'me' in what I shared. I also quite enjoyed having four hundred people listen to me talking if I'm honest! I had a good heart though and genuinely wanted people to hear what God was wanting to say. Sometimes I would approach to share and the leaders wouldn't feel it was right - it could be the timing, or the topic contrasting what else had been prophesied, for example. Maybe the word was just weird or heretical (although I don't ever remember having anything like that, I might be wrong)! However, if the fathers of the church felt it wasn't an appropriate contribution, the outcome was to undergo the 'prophetic walk of shame' - or at least, that is how I interpreted it! My insecurity flared up as I turned and headed back to my seat, imagining all four-hundred people looking at me, whispering at each other about my lack of giftedness, accuracy or some other fault. In hindsight, I now can look back and see that my inner wounds and faulty beliefs caused me to see events through a lens that coloured how I interpreted them. For the leaders of the church, who were all incredibly Godly, fatherly men, they were simply leading a meeting and aiming to hear the heart of God for that meeting. They understood the priesthood of all believers - that God speaks through all, and not just leaders - and so they empowered people to share what was on their hearts. They encouraged the risk of having people step out yet they also protected the meeting from distraction, derailment or confusion.

Because of my pain and issues though, the insecure, fearful me allowed these instances of 'rejection' to knock my confidence. My identity was so wrapped up in my gifting and how I 'performed' in that gifting, to the extent that when anything happened that caused me to think others didn't value my gift - and by extension, me. I'd go into a tailspin of self-rejection and withdrawal. That was in the early days of my faith, and I had a lot of growing up and maturing to do. Thankfully, God loves us enough to not leave us where we are at. I am convinced that He is more interested in our character than our gifting, anointing or calling. In this final section, we will look at different aspects of character that can help or hinder our prophetic ministry. Irrespective of how gifted or anointed we are, there are certain areas we do well to ensure we are stewarding well.

18. Wounds & Lies

The book of Proverbs tells us that, 'a man's gift makes room for him and brings him before the great.'[78] When someone excels at something, it attracts people. We could say that gifting opens doors. However, it is one thing for a door to be opened; it is another thing entirely for the door to remain open. It is true that gifting opens doors, but character keeps the doors open. Sometimes an individual's actions can close doors that their gifting has opened for them.

Character is a blend of our personality, traits, habits and attributes. It is shaped by both nature and nurture. It is much more than whether we are introverted or extroverted, or melancholic or sanguine. It is the manifestation of our inner health, a demonstration of who we truly are, which means that we are our truest self when no-one else is looking. Another way of defining character is thinking of it as the message we say about ourselves when we don't use words. For the Christian, it is our Christlikeness; how we line up with the standard of Jesus in every aspect of our inner man. We are all works in progress, meaning God is always changing us from the inside-out. Theologians call this process 'sanctification', which describes us taking on more and more of the character of Christ.

Godly character is something that all Christians, and therefore all prophetic people, need. If we do not have godly and mature character then our gifting - no matter how powerful or anointed -

---

78 Proverbs 18:16

will become a snare to us and can even be destructive to ourselves and those around us.

Interestingly, even the term 'prophetic' can become an identity statement or a rationale for actions, for example, "I'm not X, it's because I'm prophetic!" Really, that kind of justification for poor choices, behaviour or even sin is immaturity and will minimize the influence of such a person's ministry. We can all think of people who moved in powerful ministry, yet made some poor choices lifestyle-wise, and in effect spoiled some of the fruit of their ministry. The question of 'gifting or character?' is redundant - we need excellence in both. Gifting may come naturally to us (which is why it is gifting!) but character is the foundation from which our gifting operates, and the deepest foundations carry the biggest buildings.

Our character is positively shaped by the work of God in our lives, but it can be negatively shaped as well, most frequently through our response to negative or painful experiences. Growing up, amongst the myriad of pets we owned, for a few years we had a pet cat who we had rescued from an abusive home. He was a beautiful black cat but had certain dysfunctional behaviours that were caused by the trauma he had experienced. For example, if you looked at him and moved your hand towards him to stroke him, he recoiled back, expecting to be struck. He would also snatch food, run away with it and hide for hours, which we thought was because he was undernourished previously. Since he wasn't used to eating regularly, he would escape to eat in secret so that his food wasn't taken from him. In his mind, he did not know when the next meal would come. As a result of painful experiences in his life, his character had been affected so certain behaviours manifested as self-protection mechanisms. Everyone around him could see that his actions were extreme and unnecessary, but for him, it was about survival; he did not want to be hurt again. How we respond to pain and what we chose to believe about it will directly affect how our character develops. This is true irrespective of our physical or spiritual age. There are two main areas that we need to be aware of: wounds and lies.

Wounds

Pain hurts! Emotional pain can hurt more than some types of physical pain because it is a deeper, different kind of pain. It takes longer to subside, and medicine cannot make it go away. Things that happen to us, that are done to us, or are said to us, can inflict upon us these inner wounds which leave tender bruises on our hearts. If these sensitive spots are not healed through inner healing, counselling, Sozo, deliverance or other kinds of inner healing ministry, we begin to react to things self-protectively; we flinch or respond in a way that prevents the onset of further pain. We develop what are called coping mechanisms - behaviours designed to manage our existing pain levels, and protect against future pain. In time these behaviours become our new normal, and before we know it, we are living in such a way that doesn't deal with the root problem (the pain) but simply builds around and on top of it. Let's consider a building that has a specific purpose but is built on a foundation that in some places is broken or lacks strength or structure. There would be concern over whether or not the building is safe, and whether or not it is wise to make use of it. Limitations or repurposing would have to be implemented, or else a lot of re-digging must begin to fix the faulty foundations that the entire structure rests upon.

If we don't allow the Great Physician to heal us in the way that only He can, then our prophetic ministry will be influenced by the wounds we carry. We might not be aware of it, but many of those around us will be. In my earlier example of myself, I carried unhealed wounds of rejection due to various experiences in my life. If someone did not give me permission to prophesy at the front of our Sunday morning meeting, my pain meant I perceived it as a rejection of me as a person. This was not the truth, of course, but until I allowed healing to take place, my character was undermining my gifting and ministry. How could I function healthily in ministry if I was unable to accept authority, or if I would only ever look to lead instead of serve? God showed me that if I did not let him heal my wounds (I remain a work in progress, but am infinitely better!) it would twist the use of my gift into a self-serving source of death, rather than an other-serving source of life.

If you want to serve others in any kind of ministry, prophetic or otherwise, and seek to represent God faithfully through it, I would encourage you to ask the Father to reveal to you any pain points that He wants to heal with the oil of Holy Spirit. This is the prayer of David, to 'search me, O God, and know my heart. Try me and know my thoughts!'[79] It is likely that it might not be a quick fix - the Father is into genuine healing, not just band-aid treatment.

My experience is that deep wounds are connected to lies we are believing, which takes me to the second area that we need to be aware of that shapes our character.

Lies

Jesus said that if you "know the truth, and the truth will set you free."[80] The converse must be true then: if we don't know the truth,

---

[79] Psalm 139:23

[80] John 8:32

lies will imprison us. What we believe matters. The Apostle Paul, in writing to those crazy charismatic Corinthians a second time, tells them the same thing, 'For the weapons of our warfare are not of the flesh but have divine power to destroy strongholds. We destroy arguments and every lofty opinion raised up against the knowledge of God, and take every thought captive to obey Christ...'[81] This passage has some intriguing thoughts in it, as all of Paul's writings do!

We have weapons of warfare because as Christians we are in a war. We have an enemy who hates us and comes to steal, kill and destroy.[82] But these weapons are not of the flesh; they are not earthly, or the best of what the world or humanity has to offer. They are not ploys, schemes or trickery that have originated in the minds of men. No, they have Divine power to destroy strongholds. The introduction of a stronghold is in a negative context - it is something to be destroyed, torn down and obliterated, through weapons wielded by believers in the power of God. So strongholds are a spiritual thing. But what are they?

The Greek word for 'stronghold' is only found in the New Testament in this one location. The word can also be translated 'fortress' or even 'prison'. Historically, a stronghold was a military structure used for entrenchment i.e. holding fast onto ground and providing a place of protection and defence from opposing forces. In the book of Joshua, we can tell that the city of Jericho was a stronghold due to its walls.[83] If an army encountered a stronghold that was occupied, they

---

[81] 2 Corinthians 10:4-5

[82] John 10:10

[83] Joshua 6

would have to siege against it, which is to batter it into submission until it crumbled; or they would wait and starve out the occupants, which could take months if food supplies were abundant. Alternatively, if a stronghold was discovered empty, an army might dismantle it brick by brick so it could not be used against them. This is the imagery Paul is invoking. So we see that strongholds are spiritual places that believers need to war against. The next verse brings further clarity not only on *what* they are but *where* they are.

Paul goes on to talk about destroying arguments and lofty opinions. The word 'arguments' here comes from the Greek word *logismos,* the root of which the English word 'logic' is derived. It means to calculate, compute or reason. 'Lofty opinions' are pretentious speculations and presumptions. Together, these logics and speculations are 'raised up against...' - elevated in opposition to - 'the knowledge of God'; that is, the truth about who He is. All in all, a stronghold is a combination of internal logic and assumptions that sets itself up in contrast to the truth of who God is. It is a collection of lies and faulty beliefs that oppose God's revelation of Himself to us. A stronghold holds ground in our mind and shapes our thinking, despite it being anti-God in nature. It is a spiritual thing, so our warfare against it is to 'take every thought captive to obey Christ', i.e. to change how we think by actively addressing and confronting any thought pattern or belief that leads us away from submission to Christ. This is part of repentance, which in Greek means to change one's way of thinking, mind and therefore life. Elsewhere, Paul uses the language of 'renewal of the mind' to describe the mental process of changing our thinking that is the catalyst for a change in action.[84] A further explanation of strongholds is that they are lies that we

---

[84] Romans 12:2

believe that actively oppose the truth about God. We can believe lies in one of four areas, each of which will impact how we live.

Firstly, we can believe **lies about God Himself**. Commonly these are connected to His love, goodness, mercy, fathering of us, provision, protection, or myriad others. If we have fault-lines in our view of God, our prophetic ministry will express those fault lines because our spiritual strongholds will affect any interpretation of what we believe God may be saying. We'll have a hard time believing or representing God in His fullness in that area. If we don't believe God loves us, for example, how can we truly present the love of God sincerely and wholeheartedly to others?

Secondly, we may believe **lies about ourselves**. Understanding our identity - who we are in Christ - is so key for us as believers. If we wholly believe what God says about us, it would address a very high percentage of pastoral struggles in the church! Examples could include believing we are truly sons or daughters of God, or beliefs we have connected to areas of guilt, shame or self-worth. Interestingly enough, what we believe about ourselves is always the result of our theology. Furthermore, what we believe about God will manifest in how we see ourselves. Fear is often at the root of lies about ourselves. Paul tells the Roman church that God has given them the Spirit of sonship, not a spirit of slavery to keep them in fear.[85] In effect, as believers, whenever we are scared and have an area of fear in our life, it is because we are believing lies about the situation and not viewing it as a child of God, which brings hope and security. Rebellion, for example, can be a manifestation of a fear of being controlled. Sometimes a good question to ask ourselves - or others - is this: what are you scared of? The prophetic word is meant

[85] Romans 8:15

to tell people their destiny in God; it is about speaking identity into them. That may take the form of a reminder, an encouragement or a new revelation, but regardless of the form it takes, the prophetic word is meant to address lies we believe about ourselves or even lies others believe about us. More than once, I have been in a meeting where the mouthy, insolent, rebellious, on the verge of being kicked out of the church young man receives a prophetic word about the call of leadership God has over his life, and that word is given not just for the young man, but also for his community and leaders, so they can begin to see him how God sees him - even when he continues in his insolence or rebellion!

This example demonstrates the third type of lies that we can believe: **lies about others**. To prophesy authentically, learning to be open to how God sees others even when we don't see the same, is important, otherwise, we will begin bringing prophetic words filtered through our fleshly judgement.

Finally, the fourth type of lies we can believe is **lies about circumstances**. Again, this actually connects back to our view of God. If we don't have hope in our circumstances, then in reality, our understanding of God as Deliverer or Rescuer, for example, is lacking.

I hope that by now you can see that all lies ultimately are based on our view of God, which is why Paul told the Corinthians that strongholds set themselves up against the knowledge of God. As we learn more and more about who God is, and what He is truly like, then lies about Him will fall away, as will lies we believe about ourselves, others and circumstances. It comes back again to intimacy; the Father wants us to have first-hand accounts of His love and goodness because He really does change us from the inside-out!

Lies are undone by truth, and Jesus is the Way, the Truth and the Life.[86] God has always meant the quest for truth to be a quest after a Person.

Practising The Prophetic

Spend some time in prayerful self-reflection, asking God to show you if there are any wounds or lies in your life that He wants to minister into. Give this prayer time to 'soak in' - sometimes, God doesn't answer it immediately but may highlight something in subsequent ways. Invite Holy Spirit to bring healing and truth into those areas and let Him change you more into the image of Christ in that area. Be OK with a process that may take a bit of time, and turn it into a journey with the Father of openness, confession, intimacy and breakthrough.

---

[86] John 14:6

19. Getting in Character

To grow in the prophetic, not only do we need to increase in our ability to receive or understand revelation, but we must address any issues that will colour our understanding of those revelations. In his first letter to Timothy, Paul encouraged him to 'fan into flame the gift of God, which is in you through the laying on of my hands, for God gave us a spirit not of fear but of power and love and self-control.'[87] I believe Paul is talking here about Timothy's spiritual gifts because he connects that gift with the laying on of his hands. I don't think Paul would be talking about the gift of salvation being 'imparted' in such a way. Additionally, his exhortation to fan it into flame suggests Timothy needed to stir it up himself, so had a responsibility and involvement in utilising that gift. That doesn't sound like salvation to me. Finally, the end of the verse suggests that Timothy was scared to step out in this gift, which again fits in with the argument that Paul is talking about spiritual gifts and not the gift of salvation. Paul is encouraging Timothy to steward his spiritual gifts, and one way of doing that is to 'fan them into flame.' The Greek word used here, *anazopureo,* means to kindle up a dormant fire; revive; excite; stir up or quicken. It is an encouragement to take something that remains present but has subsided, and revitalise it through action. The imagery of a smouldering log fire being poked with an iron to stir up the flames would be fitting. Our giftings can dull and dwindle, but we can stir them up so they roar back into life.

---

[87] 2 Timothy 1:6-7

Whilst giftings dwindle, they never expire - elsewhere Paul tells the Roman church that 'the gift and calling of God are irrevocable.'[88] He is a good Father and never takes back that which, in grace, He has given. If He did, gifts and calls would be conditional on our performance, which really means they are based in works instead of grace. Giftings are part of our co-labouring with God, so we can neglect or fail to use them well. It is a kingdom principle that faithfulness leads to fruitfulness, and in the same way that neglect dulls our gifts, stewarding them well leads to growth and increase. Giftings can manifest at different intensities, and part of that is determined by how well they have been stewarded. Of course, there is the sovereign aspect of God who gives gifts to us, and He gives what He wants to whomever He wants. Some people are just 'naturally' gifted! But we can all grow and develop our gifts, whatever they are. If you ask anyone who has significant gifting in any area, they will tell you how they have developed, practised and utilised their gifts. In other words, they stewarded them and 'fanned them into flame.'

It is interesting that Paul's instructions to Timothy concerning his gifting give us the insight that Timothy's character was affecting the use of his gifts. Perhaps Timothy was a timid or fearful person by nature? We can't speculate on why he was fearful, but Paul's reminder to him that God had given him a spirit of power, love and self-control gave him three weapons to use to wage war on the Goliath of fear that he battled against. Timothy had wounds and believed some lies that ultimately were rooted in fear. This is important for us to consider: for all his gifting, imparted from the Apostle Paul himself, Timothy still needed to grow and mature in his faith. The same is true for us. There is always more for us in God.

---

[88] Romans 11:29

More Christlikeness, more fruit of the Spirit. As we grow in character, we grow in maturity. For spiritual maturity is never about gifting, but always about Christlikeness. As we mature, our gifting grows but also our understanding of how to steward and use it grows. Simply put, if we don't mature in character, not only do we lose out on the fullness of our gifting but so do the people around us.

The funny thing about maturity is that it is really hard to measure. If we measure our maturity by looking sideways and comparing ourselves to others, we potentially open up a door of pride ("I'm more mature/spiritual than *them*") or a door of self-criticism ("I'm not as spiritual as *them*"). This is another reason why community helps. Having trusted friends who are honest with us, speak into our lives - with both encouragement and challenge - and who we listen to and learn from, will always help us grow and mature. Immaturity in and of itself is not wrong - my daughter is almost three years old, and by definition is immature! She can't make her own dinner, go food shopping for us, or contribute financially in any way to the running of our household. But that's fine because that is the stage of life and season she is in. But if she was sixteen, then it would be a different matter!

Immaturity is a starting point, not a finishing point, but it is also a blind spot - we don't know when we are immature. I can think back over times in my life when I was part of teams and thought I was there to contribute my wisdom, experience and knowledge - at twenty years old - to seasoned leaders and pastors who had walked with Jesus longer than I had been alive! The reality was that in my immaturity, I failed to realise that I would do better to be quiet and learn, than talk and confirm the existence of my foolishness through my words. Looking back, I cringe a little at some of the things I said and did. Thankfully I had gracious, kind, fatherly people around me who knew when to nod and smile, when to gently correct and teach me, and when to give me a loving but honest talking to!

Immaturity is really about character. We may think that our pastor doesn't like us, or doesn't receive our prophetic ministry, or is controlling, or isn't as spiritual or anointed as we are, but in reality it could be that they see us, our gifting and character, and see some immaturity that impacts our ministry in ways we don't even realise. Every pastor I know wants healthy prophetic ministry in their church but healthy prophetic ministry must always serve the church, and therefore the leadership. That is often where perceptions differ and tensions occur.

I was approached by a gentleman I knew who wanted prophetic mentoring. He had a strong prophetic gifting, but over the years in the church he was part of, he had never felt recognised or trusted by leadership. He was frustrated and wanted to talk about it when we met. As I listened to him, he shared his disappointment at his leaders who didn't know him or see the gifting of God on him. He felt the church was missing out and wanted my advice. Knowing him, the church and the leaders, I asked him a question, "What feedback do the leaders give you about your prophetic words?" He immediately got angry and said, "They tell me I'm too long-winded and end up preaching instead of prophesying, and shouting instead of speaking. They always say this to me, it's really insulting." I suggested that if the leaders repeatedly gave that feedback to him, then this was an opportunity for growth and for building trust with them. The fact that the leaders gave him feedback showed that they saw his gifting and wanted it to be a source of life and blessing to the church. If he were to listen to them and change his ministry style accordingly, they would likely feel he was responsive to them, and therefore would be more inclined to trust him. Conversely, if he didn't, it would portray a message that he knew better than them and didn't receive their leadership. After all, they had shared this feedback with him on more than one occasion. I asked him how he would feel giving someone a voice of influence in a church he was leading if they did not respect him by considering his feedback or receiving his advice. My point to him was this: his perception of himself meant he contrasted the counsel of others against his own self-view. If they didn't line up, he dismissed the feedback. I asked him if he thought that was an immature or mature way of living. Sadly, he did not accept my input and failed to understand why I felt that any prophetic mentoring between us would ultimately be futile.

If we want to minister well in the prophetic, then as well as wanting to grow in gifting, we would do well to be as hungry, if not more so, to grow in character and maturity. Immaturity by nature is self-deceptive; we don't see it! Instead, if we think we're mature and minister from that assumption, the potential for misunderstanding and therefore conflict increases. The reality is that all of us need others. The key to moving from immaturity into maturity is teachability. How humble are we? Do we allow ourselves to be discipled? Can we accept correction? Are we easy to lead? Are we trusted by leadership? If not, why not? How can we build trust and credibility with our leaders?

Teachability is connected to how well we truly honour someone. honouring another means seeing them how God sees them. It means we then place ourselves humbly to listen and learn from them. If we don't honour someone, we won't learn from them. The converse is also true: if we don't think we can learn from our leaders, then it is fundamentally because we don't honour them.

Practising The Prophetic

Seek out a leader in your life, someone who you genuinely receive as having spiritual authority in your life. Ask them for some honest feedback, especially in the area of prophetic ministry. Ask them to tell you one thing you do well, and one way you can develop and improve. Ask them to give practical suggestions on how you can grow. Be encouraged about what they say, fight offence, and talk with God about how you can take on board the recommendations you've' received to grow in the area your leader has highlighted.

20. Six Snares

In our quest for healthy prophetic character, we can see some powerful lessons in the pages of the New Testament. Post-Pentecost, as the impact of the new covenant began to grow and the church discovered that now, all of them could be filled with Holy Spirit, no doubt there would have been excesses to deal with. Some of the New Testament writings are, in fact, responses to incorrect teaching or bad practices. Galatians, for example, is written to address an increasing legalistic influence infiltrating the church in Galatia. Another example is 1 John, which is written to believers facing the heresy of Gnosticism. Gnostics elevated the spiritual world over the material world. To the Gnostic, the spiritual realm was considered more important than the material realm, so the unseen had more value than the seen. Following this line of thinking could lead to two errors, both of which were damaging to the Gospel itself, as well as the church.

The first extreme of Gnosticism was really a false super-spirituality. There was a belief that certain special knowledge was required to grow in spirituality, which in turn generated cliques and little Gnostic clubs - with some people being inside and others outside the club. In the church, such practice would cause division through separation - something the New Testament authors frequently warned against. We can see this belief is still around today when we consider some teachings proliferated through books, websites or TV shows, that speak of heavenly secrets and revelations now being disclosed and only available for the 'anointed', 'spiritually aware' or 'spiritually tuned'. Paul told the Corinthians that 'knowledge puffs up'.[89] Whilst he was directly addressing another subject, the principle is clear: knowing things that others do not could, if not handled wisely and humbly, puff us up with pride and self-righteousness. From such a place, it isn't hard to picture someone's entire ministry, teaching and even conversation becoming centred around the special revelations they have had. The implicit - or sometimes even explicit - statement is, "I'm really spiritual because I know this and you don't, so you need to either learn from me or become like me!" It doesn't sound like a Christlike attitude conducive to healthy community!

The second extreme of the Gnostics was a logic that believed that because the spiritual was important and the material was not, it didn't matter what behaviours the Gnostics undertook involving their body; God wasn't interested in that. Such a mindset brought a false dichotomy and had the potential to lead into all sorts of immoral behaviour, not restricted to, but often, manifesting sensually or sexually. Perhaps we see a modern equivalent when we see wonderful prophetic ministry on a Sunday morning, then Monday through Saturday is a haze of ungodly language, attitudes, relationships, emotional expressions or sexuality.

Although 1 John is written in response to Gnostic influences, it has a lot to say to us about avoiding errors that will impact our character and hinder us from going deeper into the prophetic. As with many of the principles discussed in this book, they are applicable to all of us, not just those of us who seek to grow in this area of the prophetic. In my experience though, many of these pitfalls seem unusually effective in snaring those of us with a prophetic gifting. John writes to a community to give them instructions on how to discern healthy

[89] 1 Corinthians 8:1

prophetic ministry, so if we apply these instructions to ourselves, we will be able to ensure we develop our character in a healthy way.

John addresses his readers and writes, 'Beloved, do not believe every spirit, but test the spirits to see whether they are from God, for many false prophets have gone out into the world.'[90] When John uses 'spirit' here in these verses, he is referring to the possibility of teaching or revelation coming from any spirit - human, demonic or angelic. He is giving guidelines to help identify which spirit, and respond accordingly. It is interesting that he, like Paul, is totally supportive of a process of testing. He understands not every spirit, or associated teaching is from God, and seeks to protect his people. Knowing this, then, what are the signs that can help us identify healthy ministry? After all, our ministry flows from our character. What signs exist that will help us assess character in those who seek to minister prophetically, whether that is ourselves or others? There are six snares we must avoid if we want to be effective and healthy in our function. They are self-deceptive, meaning we may need the help of others to see them in our lives.

Snare 1: Hyper-Spirituality

Firstly, John simply tells his people not to believe that every revelation they hear is from God. That's pretty straightforward! As I wrote earlier, prophetic maturity involves growing in the ability to discern between what is from God and what is from us. If we don't develop this capacity, we risk embracing hyper-spirituality and confusing emotions, whims, feelings and flights of fancy with the word of the Lord. Inevitably, when we believe we hear God more often than those around us - whether we are correct in that

---

[90] 1 John 4:1

assessment or not - we will inflate our view of ourselves, and deflate our view of others.

I was working with a church to help them develop a leadership team, and there were a number of people that the senior leader felt were key leaders within the church. As I met with the people the senior leader recommended, and got to know these individuals, one person very clearly felt they were a prophet in that church. As I talked to this individual, through the language they used, it became more and more evident that to me that they believed God talked continually to them, and therefore He would have shared any new revelation for the church to them first. If anyone else in the leadership team shared an idea or thought and this person hadn't discerned it first, they rejected it out of hand because God hadn't spoken it to them! As you can imagine, this caused some consternation within the team! It also revealed a lot of spiritual pride in this individual, and some profound disrespect and dishonour towards the senior leader, who was considered 'unspiritual' and 'unanointed'. I was a spiritual leader with anointing though - but only until I began disagreeing and challenging this person! This instance illustrates the danger of hyper-spirituality both to an individual, and a community.

If we are unable, or unwilling, to weigh our revelations, or allow them to be weighed by others, we are simply demonstrating an inability to discern the source of our 'revelations'. It shows that we have a faith and lifestyle more feelings-based than Bible-based. That sounds very strong because everyone says they love the Bible, but one test is how we deal with the verses that challenge our lifestyle, opinions or theology. If we believe the book, we believe the whole book, even the parts that are challenging or make us think. Let's not just pick and choose the bits we like or understand. It is all the words of God and so deserves respect and study to understand. If we want to go deeper in the prophetic, let's be a people equally hungry to dig into scriptures, and test our revelations against the weight of the Bible.

Snare 2: Not Christ-Centred

John goes on and tells his people a way they can know healthy prophetic ministry: 'By this you know the Spirit of God: every spirit that confesses that Jesus Christ has come in the flesh is from God and every spirit that does not confess Jesus is not from God.'[91] It is amazing to me how many people who claim a prophetic ministry never talk about Jesus! Given that prophecy is relaying the heart of Jesus, it seems odd to me that for some, Jesus always wants to talk about sin, or the end of the world, or what the Devil is doing that particular moment, or what is wrong with their church, pastor or spouse! John encourages his readers to look and listen to ministry in order to answer the question: who do they say Jesus is? On an aside, John addresses the Gnostic teaching of the physical world as being lesser than the spiritual by reminding his readers that Christ came in the flesh. For a Gnostic, this is a conundrum - if the physical world is so lacking and even evil, why did God come in the form of a man, in flesh and blood and sweat and tears? Notice, too, that John doesn't just write 'Jesus', but 'Jesus Christ'. He is the Christ, the Messiah, the Anointed One. He is the God-Man, full of the power of Holy Spirit and moving in signs, wonders, miracles and the very power of God, as a model and demonstration for us. If any ministry or teaching diminishes or belittles Jesus Christ, it is not from God.

So for us, what should we do? We keep Christ central. Even when considering prophecy and other expressions of Holy Spirit, we must

---

[91] 1 John 4:2-3

always point towards Jesus Christ. His incarnation, His crucifixion, His resurrection, His ascension and His high priestly ministry are all paramount not only to ministry but to our lives. Paul told the Corinthians - those crazy, charismatic, anointed, prophetically powerful Corinthians - that the Gospel is of first importance.[92] The Gospel is the good news of Christ's life, death and resurrection, all of which were on our behalf and substitutionary in nature. His life lived for us; His death died for us; His resurrection raised for us. If the Person and works of Jesus Christ aren't our foundation, core, heart, and focus, our ministry will focus on secondary issues, which will be whatever topic tickles our ears at the time. More often than not, it seems the topics end up being spiritual warfare or end-times. To go deeper into the prophetic, let's keep the Person and work of Jesus Christ central to our life, our devotions and our ministry.

Snare 3: Worldliness

John goes on: 'They [spirits] are from the world; therefore they speak from the world and the world listens to them.'[93] The encouragement from John is to recognise what it looks like to come from the world. The Greek word for 'world' used here is *kosmos,* which in the New Testament is often used three ways: firstly, the physical world, as in the planet Earth; secondly, the population of the earth; and thirdly, the human-centred world order, i.e. society or culture apart from God.[94] So then, the signs of ministry being worldly are two-fold: first, the revelations sound the same as teachings and opinions popularised in society or culture; and second,

---

[92] 1 Corinthians 15:1-5

[93] 1 John 4:5

[94] Lehman Strauss, Demons Yes - But Thank God for Good Angels

such teachings are palatable to society at large. Being 'from the world', then, is to say the same things as the world. Scripturally, being worldly means being lukewarm - you take on the temperature of the surrounding environment until you cannot be distinguished from it. 'Worldly' revelations are those that intentionally speak from and to the flesh - they say what people want to hear, or are self-promoting and self-seeking.

We want to reach the world and be an influence within it, but this cannot be achieved by being the same as the world. Any teachings or revelations that propagate compromise aren't from God. The pattern of scripture is that God chooses a people for Himself, through whom He demonstrates His goodness and glory, and these people experience the incredible kindness and blessing of God. Other people see this, and inquire, "Why are you so blessed?" The people of God respond by pointing upwards, "It's not because of us, but because of Him!", and the nations of the world are drawn to God, so they can 'taste and see that the Lord is good!'[95]

On occasion, we can be so concerned about an error that we overcompensate and swing back against it too far. In our desire not to be worldly, let's not become so weird that we alienate people, and call it 'holiness'. Dressing oddly, speaking bizarrely and acting strangely don't represent God well. As much as we don't want the world attracted to us because we are no different to them, we also don't want the world attracted to us because we give them something to point and laugh at! The attraction the world should have to us as a people is when they see the goodness and kindness of God to us, through us and from us. We are meant to be living signposts that point to Him.

---

[95] Psalm 34:8

To go deeper in the prophetic, let's embrace a holiness and purity in our hearts and lives that demonstrate the beauty of God and showcases Him to the world. This is the goal of the prophetic ministry: to unveil the Father to a world that isn't like Him.

Snare 4: Rebellion

John continues, writing 'we [John and his associates] are from God. Whoever knows God listens to us; whoever is not from God does not listen to us. By this we know the Spirit of truth and the spirit of error.'[96]

Pretty strong, isn't it? Essentially, John is saying that those who are true ministers of God will honour his apostolic authority and spiritual leadership. If they don't, then they minister in the spirit of error! I have had experiences with self-proclaimed prophets who turn up at churches 'with a word for the church', but there is no sense of accountability, covering or authority. They just arrive and expect to be given a microphone and pulpit. Who are these people? Where do they come from? Why did they turn up that Sunday? What are they like? What will they say? What happens if they make a mess? Who would I dialogue with about it? Who has sent them to us? Who is endorsing them? What is their track record? What is their reputation in their own church? Do they have a home church? Who is their spiritual father, or mother? Why do they have crazy eyes?! Yet rather than build a relationship, credibility and trust, they will announce themselves and expect to be treated accordingly - often

---

[96] 1 John 4:6

reminding me that Jesus said that "receiving a prophet means we receive a prophet's reward."[97] The inference is clear!

It is interesting to me that when I have asked those questions - and I do, even though it feels awkward because to me it is awkward enough already so why not go all-in anyway - the response I get is a less than pleased one. You may hear phrases like 'controlling spirit', 'quenching the Spirit', and 'religious and legalistic'. My personal favourite tale is of a self-appointed prophet who disrupted a meeting because she couldn't bring her 'word', and was asked to leave. As she walked out the door, she began shouting "Ichabod[98], Ichabod, God has departed this place!" This is an extreme example, but our relationship to spiritual authority is actually a measure of our character. It takes humility to yield to someone else. Authority is entirely a biblical concept; after all, the Son submitted to the Father and the Spirit. The Trinity has both equality and submission, so counter to some teachings, they are not in opposition. Scripturally, healthy and godly authority is never enforced or imposed on another; it is always yielded and submitted to. Authority, when healthy, is given as opposed to taken. The heart of God is that we recognise Godliness in others and so give ourselves to serve them wholeheartedly.

I understand that many of us have been hurt by leadership in the past. None of us is perfect, leaders or otherwise, and many of us have made mistakes and will make mistakes! But just because something has hurt us once does not mean we should reject something God has ordained outright. In fact, one aspect of the

---

[97] John 10:41

[98] Ichabod means 'no glory', and was the name of the grandson of Eli.

Gospel that is so powerful is redemption - paying whatever price to bring something out of slavery and into liberation. Christ paid the price to rescue us from captivity and bring us into freedom. Sometimes we need to redeem some of our experiences. We pay the price - which might be the pain, the hurt, the misunderstanding, or not receiving an apology or the vindication we feel we deserve - then learn from the experience in such a way that instead of it being a source of slavery or ensnarement for us. This will mean that unforgiveness, mistrust of leaders, independence, resistance or rebellion lose any potential grip on us. We'll know we are free when we can trust our hearts and give ourselves in service to the shepherds God puts into our lives.

We grow the most when we are under a covering. No leader is perfect, so let's release our leaders from unrealistic expectations. We may be misunderstood again so let's work hard on clarifying any relational tension quickly and don't let the sun go down on our anger.[99] Sometimes we need to trust others more than we trust ourselves because they see us in a way that we can't see ourselves. If we don't work through heart wounds, then we'll always lean away from authority and not into it. You might need to repent right now of rebellion. Perhaps you need to forgive leaders - past or present. Maybe ask God to show you if there any areas that you aren't being fully submitted in. Often God shapes us through the people He puts in our lives. Depending on the people, and our response to them, that can be painful! But it is an opportunity for growth. It doesn't matter if you feel smarter, more gifted or more anointed than your leaders; God has them in your life for a reason. Consider the words of the writer of the letter to the Hebrews, who encouraged his readers to

---

[99] Ephesians 4:26

'obey your leaders and submit to them, for they are keeping watch over your souls, as those who will have to give an account.'[100]

Our relationship to spiritual authority will certainly have an effect on our prophetic growth. It is a character issue. Let's not confuse freedom with independence, or claim that feedback is control. Being unwilling to be under authority figures who can speak into our lives will hinder our prophetic growth. To go deeper in the prophetic, let's locate and live under a genuine spiritual covering, allowing leaders to lead us and being vulnerable and teachable towards them.

Snare 5: Independence

John continues his first letter by writing 'Beloved, let us love one another, for love is from God, and whoever loves has been born of God and knows God.'[101] John loves to talk about love, but for love to truly be love, it requires an object of that love. John states who we are meant to love: one another.

'One another' is plural, and suggests a relational connection, which tells me that he is talking about community. In the New Testament, community is the great check and balance that protects against error, protects the weak, and teaches the immature. If we aren't part of community, we cannot enjoy the benefits of community. God has always had a heart to have a people that declare His praise[102] - in other words, showcase what He is like to the world. This people are the Church, who declare the manifold wisdom of God to rulers and

---

[100] Hebrews 13:17

[101] 1 John 4:7

[102] Isaiah 43:17

authorities in the Heavenly places.[103] The idea is that community shapes us, and we shape community. After all, our giftings are not for us but are for others around us. Yet again, if we are not part of the corporate, how can we be blessed or be a blessing? Biblically, being part of community is not simply attending meetings; it is sharing life together. There are numerous 'one anothering' verses in the New Testament - encourage one another, love one another, rebuke one another, forgive one another, and many others - that suggest that this community of believers, the church, is one of God's big new covenant ideas. It is interesting to me that the sign of remembrance of the New Covenant - the Lord's Supper, Communion, the bread and wine - is a meal, which suggests family and community. It involves others. Knowing others and being known matters. Community, when embraced genuinely and authentically, shapes and changes us. It sanctifies us, making us more like Christ. There are many occasions in my life when a brother or sister in Christ has challenged, corrected, taught, encouraged, rebuked or comforted me just when I've needed it. Family matters.

When it comes to prophetic ministry, the people we practice on at first had better be those we are in community with! They can extend grace, mercy and encouragement as we learn and grow. As we mature and grow, recognition and trust comes, which increases opportunities and influence, which can lead to further growth. I'm not suggesting we should only be in community to practice on people, but if you are in community and practising on people, beware using them as projects or they will let you know about it!

Community will knock our rough edges off. If we have funny prophetic habits, or strange delivery, or revelations that don't make

---

103 Ephesians 3:10

sense, then they will help us grow. The church is a gift of grace to the individual believer. We were never meant to live independently, but interdependently. Paul uses the illustration of a body in 1 Corinthians 12 for a reason; every part different and unique, yet connected, with the same aim, under the same head. Let's be connected and playing our part. Let's locate and live in a genuine spiritual community, allowing others to love us while we remain vulnerable and teachable towards them, as we are with our leaders. In doing so we will grow in both gifting and character.

Snare 6: Lack of Love

John challenges his people by stating, 'Anyone who does not love does not know God, because God is love.'[104] The fruit of our friendship with God should be love - love for God, love for other believers, and love for the lost. In fact, a lack of love in the life of a believer is a worrying sign, because God changes us more and more into the image of Christ. His character becomes our character, and His character is Love. The Apostle Paul himself writes to the prophetically gifted Christians to remind them that love is paramount, and without love, no prophecy or knowledge or faith matters.[105]

God is love, so it follows that everything He says and does is love. Why, then, should there ever be a contradiction between the heart of God and the hearts of those who claim to speak on His behalf? The more we let God change us, the more we take on the image of Christ. That means that we cannot help but grow in love. The Apostle Paul knew this because his experience of the Love of God had met him as

---

[104] 1 John 4:8

[105] 1 Corinthians 13:1

a zealous religious fundamentalist searching for those he considered heretics to execute or imprison, and changed him into a leader, evangelist and teacher of the very faith he had sought to eradicate. Love does that to people; it captivates, compels and transforms them. Love wins.

The Apostle John, in the gospel that he wrote, often referred to himself as 'the disciple that Jesus loved.' To me, that phrase contains a dual sense of wonder - wonder that a man like himself could draw close to the Son of God and be known fully, and wonder that this Son of God would fully know John and love him anyway. Elsewhere in his first letter, John wrote, 'by this we know love, that He [Jesus Christ] laid down His life for us...'[106] If we want to know what love is, we must consider the Cross of Christ. The self-sacrifice of Christ is the most loving act in the whole of human history. If it is the standard of love, it is the very definition of love. Therefore we know that true, authentic, real love is sacrificial. It, by nature, involves death - the death of personal agenda, personal gain, and even things that may be beneficial or pleasurable to us. Because Jesus died for others and not for Himself, we can see that love is focused on others; it is not self-centred. Love is not manipulative or controlling but seeks to serve others in such a way that the person acting in love would do so even to their own detriment. Love has to involve action; it demands movement. Real love is not satisfied with feelings or words but manifests itself through doing. Love is a verb, and Christ shows us this through His actions.

Christ laid down his life for us when we were sinners. At our worst state, in a condition wholly unacceptable to God, when we were enemies of God and fundamentally separated by Him because of our

[106] 1 John 3:16

own sin, Christ still loved us. His love was, and remains, not conditional on our performance or state. At our lowest, He acted. Love that only serves certain types of people, or only is available when people attain a certain standard or develop a specific quality, is not love.

When we consider the love of Christ for us, it cannot help but change us, and it will change our ministry. How we prophesy will be different. A prophetic ministry that has a lack of love is not representing the heart of God well and should be something we seek to avoid.

Practising The Prophetic

Look over the six character snares in this chapter - hyper-spirituality, not being Christ-centred, worldliness, rebellion, independence, and lack of love. In which areas are you strongest, and in which ones are you weakest? Perhaps ask a close friend or leader for their opinion. Make a prayerful commitment to develop the one you feel you need to grow in the most.

21. Keeping the River Clean

As well as attitudes in our character, there can be certain actions that affect our prophetic ministry. Of course, prophecy is a gift of grace and so revelation is dependent on God speaking and our ability to discern and interpret it. We can't earn or lose the ability to receive revelation. But certainly, there can be things we do that affect our ability to see, hear or feel what God is saying. Think of it like a stream of water; we can have a perfectly pure brook that is crystal-clear and free from any kind of impurity, or the water can be polluted with toxins, brown and dirty, or various stages in between.

Paul told the Roman church that the 'kingdom of God is... righteousness, peace and joy in the Holy Spirit.'[107] This verse tells us the character of the kingdom because it is the character of the King. The Kingdom of God is the realm of God's rule; it is anything, anywhere or anyone who is under His dominion and in His domain. He is seeking to expand His kingdom's rule but this creates a tension; in one sense, the kingdom of God has arrived - Jesus said that it was at hand[108] - and yet we can see that it is not yet in its fullness, because heaven and earth are not yet aligned. In the Lord's Prayer, Jesus prayed, "Our Father in Heaven, hallowed be Your name. Your kingdom come, Your will be done on earth as it is in

---

[107] Romans 14:17

[108] Mark 1:15

Heaven..."[109] From this, we can see that Jesus equated the will of God being fulfiled, the Kingdom of God coming (meaning arriving or increasing) and earth becoming more like Heaven. Yet we can all see that there are things on earth that are not in Heaven, and things in Heaven that are not yet on earth. The Apostle John had a revelation that the new heavens and new earth - the place where the Kingdom of God is fully realised - would be a place where God will 'wipe away every tear from their eyes, and death shall be no more neither will there be mourning, nor crying, nor pain anymore, for the former things have passed away.'[110] We can all agree that whilst there still exists sadness, sickness, poverty, injustice and death on the earth - things that are not in Heaven - we as Christians, and therefore the Church, still have a mission to fulfil.

Therefore, because we live in this tension of a Kingdom 'now and not yet', we ourselves are in the Kingdom but areas of our lives may still be under enemy influence. This is the nature of spiritual warfare; the enemy attempts to gain influence over us through intimidation or deception, so he can invade an area of our life and gain a foothold. We relinquish authority to him whenever we fall for one of his schemes. Paul's description of God's kingdom showed the Roman church the fruit of the Kingdom of God, so they could recognise what it looked like to partner with God's way of doing things.

If these three characteristics of righteousness, peace and joy reveal the heart of the kingdom of light, then the opposite fruit to these must show the kingdom of darkness. It follows that the presence of these kingdom traits, or their opposites, will impact us, and therefore

[109] Matthew 6:9-10

[110] Revelation 21:4

our 'prophetic river'. Let's take a few moments to consider these traits of 'righteousness, peace and joy in the Holy Spirit', and the contrasting values.

Righteousness versus Impurity

As I wrote earlier, 'righteousness' is alignment with the standards of Heaven that God has set. This means that anything that does not align with those standards is 'unrighteous.' Impurity is unrighteous because God makes it clear that His people are not to be like the world when it comes to expressions of sexuality. How we address lust and sexual sin is important. Pornography is one such sexual sin, as are inappropriate relationships whether physical or emotional. It is my conviction that what we choose to look at - or 'see' - will affect our thought life, which in turn could impact us when it comes to hearing from God. Thankfully, God's mercy is available every day and His kindness is never exhausted for us, even when we sin, stumble and fall.

Peace versus Brokenness

The biblical concept of peace is much more than the absence of conflict. The Greek word Paul uses is *eirene*, which encompasses not only a lack of hostility but also a state of order and rest that lead to the blessings of prosperity. It is the Greek equivalent of the Hebrew word *shalom*. In contrast, the opposing trait is 'brokenness', which describes an internal warring within ourselves that prevents us from living wholly. It encompasses any emotional wounds and lies that hinders us from living peacefully with ourselves, with others or with God. Such inner turmoil will cause us to use our gifting to attempt to create a false peace, which seeks to placate rather than truly reconcile. Healthy ministry flows from a place of peace within us and reproduces such peace outside of us.

Unforgiveness is another area that opposes peace because, by nature, unforgiveness is choosing to live in a state of war with another person. Biblically, the Apostle Paul often links the subject of forgiveness with the cross of Christ, as if to say 'if we've been forgiven all of our sin by God, why are we not forgiving someone else for theirs?' Jesus links unforgiveness many times with torment, suggesting that it is an open door to demonic attack. Ultimately, if we do not live in peace, we risk interpreting revelation through a fractured lens. Whether we need to undergo some inner healing or forgive those who have offended us, a life of peace is the will of God for us, who sent the Prince of Peace to make it available.

Joy versus Fear

Psalm 16 tells us that in God's presence, there is 'fullness of joy', and 'at [God's] right hand are pleasures evermore'.[111] One of the natural effects of walking with God and experiencing Him is joy, which shows itself in the life of the believer through delight, celebration, gratitude and wonder. In contrast, the enemy loves to use fear to rob us of the blessings that come from knowing God. Fear is a kind of faith; instead of being God-focused, it is circumstance-focused. Fear has been defined as 'false expectations assumed real'. When we think the worst and live from a place believing that the worst-case scenario has, is or will happen, we lose joy and peace is killed, and we can accommodate or make space for fear by calling it 'worry' or 'anxiety'. Fear influences what we see, and it can be an open door for the enemy to speak to us with lies and deceit to further ensnare us.

---

[111] Psalm 16:11

Particular types of fear that carry a potency in the area of the prophetic are the fear of failure and fear of man. The fear of failure can be rooted in perfectionism - having to get it right first time, every time, the whole time, or our self-worth crumbles because of our self-critiqued performance - or fear of rejection. Fear of failure is the enemy of risk-taking, which is a core foundation on which prophetic ministry is built. If we are too scared to step out in faith and take risks by sharing what we see, hear or feel, we will not prophesy, and the benefit of those words will never be realised.

The fear of man comes when we are more concerned with the opinions of people than the opinion of God. Sometimes, the fear of man is connected to low self-esteem or self-worth; we don't see ourselves how God sees us, and so reduce our lives to the level of the lies we believe about ourselves. For example, if I don't think I'm good enough for God to speak through, then guess what - I won't let God speak through me.

On other occasions, the fear of man can be connected to our environment, especially if we are ministering in situations where we encounter either a religious spirit or a political spirit. These are human, fleshly, soulish mindsets and strongholds that may be present in others, or even present in ourselves. Like all strongholds, they are self-deceptive, meaning it takes God to reveal when we have one!

A religious spirit is predominantly occupied with what God requires. Someone with a religious spirit can have a black-and-white view of who God is and how He works. They will struggle with any understanding of God or expression of the work of the Spirit that differs from what they have decided is correct. These people often have a high value for truth and holiness so will be strong scripturally - or at least, in their interpretation and understanding of the scriptures. Whilst they may appear rigid and legalistic, they will have a real heart for purity, righteousness and justice. Such people may battle internally with performance and working for God's love, while silently struggling with judgmentalism or guilt and shame at not making the grade they believe they need to live up to. Of course, they know what the truth is but will not necessarily recognise that what they say and how they live do not match up. In many ways, the Pharisees encompassed the characteristics of the religious spirit. If we are fearful of those with a religious spirit or have one ourselves, we will fit our prophetic ministry into the cage created by others' restrictive views. In fact, one of the roles of the prophetic ministry is to truly unveil the heart of God, which can at times offend the religious. This does not mean that we should behave offensively and label any attempted correction as 'religious', but it does mean that to truly represent God, there may well be times that we challenge others' preconceptions of who He is and how He works.

A political spirit is focused on its own agenda, ambitions and goals. It seeks to advance that agenda whatever the cost, and can be covert or overt depending on the situation and its influence. Someone with a political spirit will seek to orchestrate outcomes within a group of people because they are hungry for power so they seek positions of authority not to serve others, but to serve themselves. Whether they think they are doing the right thing or not, they will use various tools to achieve their own ends: seduction; flattery; intimidation; manipulation; deceit; peer pressure; or even the creation of a false peace that is really an unhealthy compromise that sacrifices principles and prepares the ground for later control. The challenge of the prophetic ministry, when faced with political spirits, is that often the agenda of God is different from the agenda of man. If we are fearful, will we speak out? How will we deal with opposition? Of course, we should not label any questioning of our revelations as 'political', but it does mean that to truly represent God, there may well be times where we are required to say the unpopular thing. Naturally, how we say it can be wise or it can be foolish!

In summary, both the religious and political spirits are about control. The religious seeks to control how people relate to God, and the political looks to control how people relate to other people. Control is really a manifestation of fear; it comes from a place of fear that bad things will happen, so action must be taken to prevent them. These actions take the form of an overdeveloped sense of protection, either of self (we control what happens around us to protect ourselves from pain), or others (we control what others can and cannot do, and how they can do them, because we want the best for them, so we try to make things happen in accordance with our plans). Control feels like feeling responsibility for something or someone, but actually, it is disempowering, dishonouring and quenching.

To reiterate, prophecy influenced by mindsets of religion, politics or control comes from a place of fear. Prophecy seeks to expand the hearer's relationship with God, relationship with others, and personal experience of freedom to be themselves in the way God made them. Conversely, fear seeks to restrict someone in their walk with God, walk with others, and the ability to be themselves. John told his followers that 'perfect love casts out fear.'[112] Fear has no place in the hearts of those of us who seek to prophesy well and must be crushed. The antidote to fear is first, repentance, and second, experiencing the love of God more and more, so it melts away the shadow of fear.

---

[112] 1 John 4:18

Holy Spirit versus Unclean Spirits

Because we are spiritual beings, we can access the spirit realm. But not everything from the spirit realm is godly! Drinking from other fountains of revelation will pollute us; we are to be people filled with the Holy Spirit, not influenced by evil or unclean spirits. There are many warnings in scripture, for example, about the dangers of occultic practices:

'When you come into the land which the Lord your God gives you, you shall not learn to follow the abominable practices of those nations. There shall not be found among you anyone who burns his son or his daughter as an offering, anyone who practices divination or tells fortunes or interprets omens or a sorcerer or a charmer or a medium or a necromancer or one who inquires of the dead, for whoever does these things is an abomination to the Lord. And because of these abominations the Lord your God is driving them out before you.'[113]

That's pretty clear! Isn't it interesting that in the eyes of God, when He begins listing abominable practices, the first one He condemns is child sacrifice by way of burning the child alive? This was an act of worship carried out by the Canaanite people to their demonic gods, but you'd be hard pressed nowadays to find someone in their right mind who would be okay with committing or endorsing such a practice; almost everyone would admit that such a thing is an evil, abominable action that should be stamped out. But the list of practices that follow this disgusting act may perhaps not seem so extreme, especially in today's society. Many of these activities overlap or can be used interchangeably, but at their root is either

---

113 Deuteronomy 18:9-12

divination, which is any attempt to discover hidden knowledge or the future, or sorcery, which is the use of spells to influence events or people. The practices in this passage encompass many prolific actions such as horoscopes, fortune-telling, magic and seances, as well as many others. In God's eyes, these are listed alongside child sacrifice!

It is interesting also to note that these aforementioned occultic activities are the counterfeit of the prophetic gifts - both the forthtelling (revealing the hidden present) and foretelling (revealing the unknown future) aspects of prophecy. Ultimately, occultic activities have one of two aims; they are either intended to gain control over events or gain control of people. Both aims are about obtaining power illicitly and are therefore counter to God's ways. By carrying out such acts, a person is elevating themselves into a role that is reserved only for God and is, therefore, an act of rebellion against Him. This is confirmed by the prophet Samuel who told King Saul that 'rebellion is as the sin of divination',[114] which not only tells us that illicit practices of divining the unknown are a big deal to God, but He places rebellion on the same level as the occult, and therefore child sacrifice!

Fortunately, we can repent of occultic involvement, whether current or historic and renounce our connection to it. Additionally, if this is an area that we have been drawn to before, even if we have not been practising any kind of dark activity for a while, it is wise to take a quick audit with the Lord and ensure that the motive of the heart that drew us that way has been addressed. It might have been a desire for power, or control, or curiosity, but whatever it is, if it has not been

---

[114] 1 Samuel 15:23

dealt with, it could still potentially be an issue that could impact our ministry.

Practising The Prophetic

Look over the four 'pollutants' in this chapter - impurity, brokenness, fear and the occult. In which areas are you strongest, and in which ones are you most vulnerable to? Do any have a foothold or influence in your life? Confess it, renounce it, make a fresh dedication of yourself to the Lord, and seek wise counsel from leaders how to push past this challenge with the support of community.

22. Growth Engines

Much success is built on discipline, habits and routines. It has been said that it takes many years of practice to be an overnight success! Growth takes time, and healthy growth is often slow growth. We've seen snares and pollutants to avoid, but what disciplines or practices can we incorporate into our own lives to help us grow in the prophetic gifts? What proactive and practical steps can we take to invest in our gifting and maximise our growth?

Firstly, **cultivating a deep friendship with God**. In the sermon on the mount, Jesus told us that 'blessed are the pure in heart, for they will see God.'[115] Whilst this can, and does, mean purity on a moral level, it also means a purity of heart that is not contaminated or spoiled by other concerns - in a sense, a heart singly focused and desiring of one thing alone. Our hunger for God will show itself not in the public demonstration of gifts or abilities, but in the quest for intimacy through prayer and worship. As we hunger for God, our pursuit of Him will increase. He reveals Himself to those who genuinely seek Him,[116] rewarding them with the gift of Himself,[117] and our intimacy with Him, and therefore friendship, grows. God loves friendship with people; Abraham was called a friend of God[118]

---

[115] Matthew 5:8

[116] Hebrews 11:6

[117] James 4:8

[118] James 2:23

because of the trust and faith Abraham placed in Him. The same was said of Moses, who spoke face to face with God as men do with their friends.[119] What an incredible privilege, now available to us in this new covenant. Friends share their hearts, so we should not be surprised that one way to grow in the prophetic is to cultivate a genuine, authentic friendship with God.

Secondly, keep on being **filled with Holy Spirit**. Paul encouraged the people in the Ephesian church to '...be filled with the Spirit...'[120] The Greek word for 'filled' here is in a present tense, indicating that Paul is suggesting an ongoing experience. It is not a passive thing, but active - it is something we actually do. You could say that Paul is encouraging the Ephesians to 'keep on being filled with the Spirit'. As we allow Him to fill us, there will be an overflow, just like Jesus said - out of us, streams of living water will flow.[121] This flow could take many forms, but one form will be prophecy. This is confirmed with the account in Acts 2, which saw the disciples filled with the Spirit and then prophesying. Simply put, as we experience the Presence and Power of God through encounters with Holy Spirit, His fruit and gifts will flow.

Thirdly, **walk in step with the Spirit.** It is one thing to be filled with the Spirit, but He dwells within us for a purpose. In the Old Testament, people would sometimes be anointed with oil as a sign of commissioning for a particular purpose. In the New Testament, we are all anointed, and Holy Spirit is the oil of anointing. Anointing is

---

[119] Exodus 33:11

[120] Ephesians 5:18

[121] John 7:38

a mysterious thing, but we all know it when we see it! We make a mistake when we talk about anointing as an abstract, impersonal force. The anointing is a Person, not just a power - but the Person has power! He - Holy Spirit - gives us all we need to fulfil the purpose of God assigned to us. In that sense, anointing describes the effectiveness of the partnership between Holy Spirit and Man.

To grow in anointing is to grow in relationship with Holy Spirit. Jesus said it was better for Him to leave so He could send the Spirit.[122] He did not want us left alone in the world but instead connected to the Helper who would live within us. Another name for Holy Spirit is the Comforter. So we begin to see that this is a relationship of intimacy, full of help and comfort. Scripture tells us that we can grieve Holy Spirit,[123] meaning we can make God sad with our actions!

It is the role of Holy Spirit to help us live our new spiritual life, teaching us all that Jesus said, and applying the work of the grace of God to our lives. This means that our partnership with Him is essential for a successful Christian life. Paul told the Galatian church, who were struggling with legalistic and religious influences within them, that living life purely by the law of God was demeaning the Gospel. Instead, he encouraged them that if we 'live by the Spirit, let us also keep in step with Spirit.[124] Like a dance, we keep close to Him, following His lead. We let Him set the direction, tempo and rhythm, and respond by working with Him and not against Him. Dancing is intimate because bodies are close, cheeks

---

[122] John 16:7

[123] Ephesians 4:30

[124] Galatians 5:25

touch and eyes connect. Keeping in step with the Spirit means watching, listening and following instructions in the same way Jesus modelled for us when He said that He 'only does what He sees the Father doing'.[125]

Fourthly, we cannot grow in the prophetic without **taking risk**. Sometimes an opportunity for stepping out in risk will come when we see a moment that is ripe for us to do something we aren't quite comfortable doing but know it is what the situation needs. Other times, you may feel God give you a nudge and invite you to trust not only Him but particularly in your ability to hear Him! The reality is that growth is spelt R.I.S.K. It's true of anything; we only grow in something when we push past what is comfortable into new ground. When the new ground becomes our new normal, we've grown! If we stay there for too long, we'll plateau - but God has an excellent track record of bringing us into situations that challenge any stagnancy we may have embraced! Fear is the only thing that will stop us from taking risks. But there is no other way around it; if we want to see things we've never seen, we need to do things we've never done. There is encouragement, however! Remember Peter, who denied to a servant girl that he knew Christ?[126] That same Peter, at Pentecost, gets filled with the Holy Spirit in Acts 2 and stands up before a great number of people, preaching the Gospel, unafraid of who sees him. Three thousand are saved that day! The answer to fear? Get filled with the Holy Spirit again.

Fifthly, keep **practising the prophetic**. As you've been reading, perhaps you've identified some forms of revelation - seeing, hearing

---

[125] John 5:19

[126] John 18

or sensing - that you know God uses to speak to you. Learn to recognise when revelation is coming, and act on it. Be prepared to prophesy or share words of knowledge whether you are in a church setting, or at work, or even in a public place. Whether we are ministering to a believer or a non-believer, in a church meeting or a shop, the skill-set and process are the same.

Sixthly, **form prophetic partnerships**. The Old Testament tells us about companies of prophets - groups of people who banded together and prophesied.[127] In one example, the prophet Samuel was head of the company, suggesting there were disciples, and the company was like a school.[128] No doubt this group would have helped individuals grow in their prophetic ministry through community, accountability and training. If this was a good idea in the Old Testament, then why not in the New? Get together with like-minded individuals to train, sharpen and encourage each other. Practise prophesying in pairs or as a group. Request feedback on words - not just about the accuracy, but the delivery too. Intercede together for individuals, your leaders, community and anything else God brings to mind.

One caution though: I've seen prophetic groups form together that became elitist and looked down on people who were not part of the group, including the pastors and church leaders. They had set themselves up as uninvited consultants to the leaders, prophesying advice or claiming to discern what was really going on in the spiritual life of the church. Don't do that! If you want to form a prophetic team, keep accountable to your leaders and involve them in the process and formation of the group. Any healthy church leader

---

[127] 1 Samuel 19:18-24; 2 Kings 2; 2 Kings 4:38-44

[128] 1 Samuel 19:20

would love to have a powerful, anointed team full of gifted and mature prophetic people, exemplary in character, who are asking how they can serve and be a blessing! Be that group and not any other kind. The prophetic ministry is there to serve, after all.

Practising The Prophetic
Look over the six 'growth engines' in this chapter - friendship with God, being filled with the Spirit, walking in step with the Spirit, taking risk, practising the prophetic and forming prophetic partnerships. Which ones stand out to you that if started, would bring growth to you? Find someone to be accountable with, and start doing it!

Conclusion

The Bible is clear that spiritual gifts and revelations are not an endorsement of our spirituality. Fruit is; gifts are not. Additionally, *how* God speaks to us is not a reason for boasting - it doesn't matter what or how you see, hear or feel. The most important thing is ensuring we hear Him accurately then faithfully communicate Him, in an honourable manner. The Apostle Paul, writing to the gifted, prophetic, charismatic, anointed, supernatural Corinthian church, wrote 'If I have prophetic powers, and understand all mysteries and all knowledge, and if I have all faith, so as to remove mountains, but have not love, I am nothing.'[129]

Get love: Love *for* God, love *from* God, and love *for* others. *Then* prophesy.

---

[129] 1 Corinthians 13:2

About the Author

Anthony Hilder is an organisational consultant, husband, father, leader, teacher, coach, speaker and writer. He has an extensive leadership background in business, Christian ministry and coaching.

He is originally from the U.K., has lived and worked in the United States, and now lives in Scotland with his wife Katie, daughter Sophie and son Ross.

Anthony is passionate about seeing people and organisations fulfil their unique purpose, and loves to partner with them in developing the knowledge, beliefs and skills they need to do so.

You can find out more about Anthony and his work at **www.anthonyhilder.com.**

Sign up for exclusive offers and updates of new releases from the author at **www.anthonyhilder.com/writing**

29166715R00110

Printed in Poland
by Amazon Fulfillment
Poland Sp. z o.o., Wrocław